WORDS IN THE MIND

WORDS IN THE MIND

EXPLORING SOME EFFECTS OF
POETRY, ENGLISH AND FRENCH

By

Charles Davy

HARVARD UNIVERSITY PRESS
CAMBRIDGE, MASSACHUSETTS
1965

First published 1965

© Charles Davy 1965

Library of Congress Catalog Card Number: 65-23723

Printed in Great Britain

ACKNOWLEDGMENTS

The authorized English translations of the works of Paul Valéry vest exclusively in Bollingen Foundation, New York. Their permission to publish Mr. Davy's translations of *Le Cimetière Marin* and *La Jeune Parque* is gratefully acknowledged. Thanks are also due to Mrs. Helen Thomas and Faber & Faber Ltd. for permission to reprint Edward Thomas's poem *Tall Nettles*.

CONTENTS

Preface

WHILE trying to translate Paul Valéry's two long poems, *Le Cimetière Marin* and *La Jeune Parque*, I read most of his prose writings on poetry and explored the Symbolist background of his youth. A great deal has of course been written about this period and its later influence on English poetry, but I found it leading me to look at the modern history of poetry in relation to the evolution of human consciousness, and that is less familiar ground.

Poetry was once taken as an inspiration from a god. But

> The laurels all are cut
> The bowers are bare of bay
> That once the Muses wore. . . .

Or, as I. A. Richards put it in a well-known passage forty years ago: "The central dominant change may be described as the *Neutralisation of Nature*, the transference from the Magical View of the world to the scientific. . . . The beliefs in Inspiration and the beliefs underlying ritual are representative parts of this view. . . . There is some evidence that Poetry, together with the other Arts, arose with the Magical View. It is a possibility to be seriously considered that Poetry may pass away with it."

For one effect of this change, Richards argued (he might phrase it differently now) has been that many of the statements which poetry seems to make about the world are no longer acceptable to a well-informed mind; they are seen to be false.

We shall go further into this; the 'central dominant change' is certainly one reason for the uneasy relationship between poetry and modern science. But there is another, more intimate reason, connected with language. For poetry continues to use language in ways that can have something like a 'magical' effect;

9

not only a communicative but an operative effect, which can be felt in the head and seems to open a window in the mind. A scientific critic who responds to poetry must recognise this effect, but it is not easily translatable into scientific terms.

The sort of questions that arise are: What is poetry, apart from its discursive meaning, about? What does it communicate? How does it influence our apprehension of the world? These questions have been in the background of controversy ever since the 'central dominant change' set in; ever since the Utilitarians attacked poetry as useless and Keats feared that science was going to "conquer all mysteries by rule and line". They were a main issue among the Symbolists, and since the emergence in the twenties of the Anglo-American 'new poetry' and 'new criticism', a formidable apparatus has been brought to bear on them. But in my belief they have not been altogether answered, so in this essay I have tried, not to offer any final answer, but to approach them in the light of two rather neglected factors—the evolution of consciousness and the action of words on the mind.

Finally, I try to widen the issue by asking in what ways the arts in general will be needed, and what sort of background they will need, in the technological civilisation of the very near future.

As to the translations, Valéry's poetry will outlast his writings about poetry. Hence it seemed incongruous to discuss his poetics without endeavouring to convey some impression of him as a poet. Not that translations can do much, for poetry (it hardly needs saying again) is strictly untranslatable. Perhaps the only useful translations are literal ones for students. But a poem in another language may impel someone to attempt a rendering of it in his own tongue, as Valéry's poems often have done, particularly *Le Cimetière Marin* (I have not come upon a published rendering of *La Jeune Parque* in English verse, though one may exist somewhere). A translator of Valéry can hope he has given some idea of the kind of poet Valéry is; but his wish to make the attempt is his only unassailable excuse.

C.D.

PART I

RHYME AND REASON

I

"Manoeuvre of Myself"

No other poet has written so much about the writing of poetry as Valéry did, and no other considerable poet has been so apparently indifferent towards his own work.

In 1922, at the height of his reputation, he wrote to André Gide: "They want me to represent French poetry. They take me for a poet. I don't give a damn for poetry! It interests me only by accident. It is only by accident that I have written verses. I should be exactly the same if I hadn't written them. This means that in my own eyes I should be worth exactly the same. For me, all that has no importance."[1]

No doubt these words were partly stung out of Valéry by the boring exactions of a public literary career. But he often made similar remarks. He seemed to feel that for anyone who prized, as he did, scientifically disciplined thinking, poetry could have value only as an occasional private pleasure and as an exercise for the poet. And in his Preface to an *Anthologie des Poètes de la N.R.F.* (1936), he wrote: "From the remotest antiquity to the present time, reading and writing have been the sole means of exchange and the only methods of developing and preserving expression through language. One can no longer answer for their future. As for minds, one already sees that they are wooed and captured by so much immediate magic, so many direct stimuli, which with no effort provide the most intense sensations and show them life itself and the whole of nature, that one may doubt whether our grandchildren will find the slightest savour in the outdated graces of our most extraordinary poets and of poetry in general."[2]

[1] André Gide, *Journal 1889–1939* (Gallimard, 1948), p. 749
[2] From 'The Problems of Poetry', translated in *Paul Valéry: The Art of Poetry*, volume seven of *The Collected Works of Paul Valéry*, edited by Jackson

Thus Valéry joins those who from Keats onwards have asked whether there is any future for poetry in a scientific age. I want to approach this question through some of the paradoxes of Valéry's life.

*   *   *

At the age of eighteen, while he was living at Montpellier, near the little Mediterranean port of Sète where he had been born in 1871, Valéry wrote a short essay, *Sur la Technique Littéraire*. It opens: "Literature is the art of playing on the minds of others," and it goes on to speak of "a totally new conception of the poet. He is no longer the dishevelled madman who writes a whole poem in the course of one feverish night; he is a cool scientist, almost an algebraist, in the service of a subtle dreamer."[1]

In this essay, too, occurs the first of Valéry's tributes to Poe ("the extremely original poetic theory of Edgar Poe"); and soon afterwards, in his first letter to Mallarmé, he declared himself "profoundly penetrated by the learned doctrines of the great Edgar Allen Poe—perhaps the most subtle artist of this century". Here, he perhaps felt, was a man who had done what he hoped to do—who had combined the study of science with the practice of poetry and had brought it off with remarkable success. Thus in *The Philosophy of Composition* Poe professes to describe the method of 'calculated effects' whereby he had composed *The Raven* (which certainly makes an effect, though on me a maddening one). Later—Valéry may never have heard of this—Poe seems to have admitted that he had worked out the theory only after writing the poem.[2]

Mathews (New York, Bollingen Foundation; London, Routledge, 1958). This volume (henceforward referred to as *A.P.*) brings together in English versions, with an Introduction by T. S. Eliot, an excellent selection of Valéry's prose writings on poetry.

[1] *A.P.*, p. 315
[2] See *Poe's Complete Poetical Works, with Three Essays on Poetry,* edited by R. Brimley Johnson (Oxford University Press, 1909)

The well-known admiration felt for Poe's poetry by the French Symbolists, from Baudelaire onwards, has always seemed to English readers very odd; the best comment on it, perhaps, is by Aldous Huxley: "A taint of vulgarity spoils, for the English reader, all but two or three of his poems—the marvellous *City in the Sea* and *To Helen*, for example, whose beauty and crystal perfection make us realise, as we read them, what a very great artist perished on most of the occasions when Poe wrote verse. It is to this perished artist that the French poets pay their tribute. Not being English, they are incapable of appreciating those finer shades of vulgarity that ruin Poe for us, just as we, not being French, are incapable of appreciating those finer shades of lyrical beauty which are, for them, the making of La Fontaine."[1]

This was certainly true (ironically) of Poe himself. "It must be observed," he remarks, "that the French language is strangely peculiar on this point—*that it is without accentuation, and consequently without verse*. . . . Comparatively, the French have no verse worthy of the name—which is the fact, put in sufficiently plain terms."

However, the Symbolists could always believe that Poe would have changed his opinion if he could have read their new poetry; and one can see why his theories of composition made such an impression on them, given their response to his verse. Not only had Poe discovered a new and ostensibly scientific method of writing poetry; he had proved that his method could yield wonderful results.

Valéry's own high regard for Poe was much more than a youthful enthusiasm. In 1924, at the age of fifty-three, he could still write: "Never until Poe had the problem of literature been studied in terms of its premises, reduced to a problem of psychology, tackled by an analytic method in which the logic and mechanics of its effects were deliberately employed. For the first time, the relations between the work and the reader were

[1] From 'Vulgarity in Literature' in *Music at Night* (collected edition, Chatto and Windus, 1949)

elucidated and laid down as the positive foundations of art."[1]

Yet it was soon after encountering Poe that the young Valéry lost interest in writing poetry. Perhaps he felt that his own early verses had been written in a way that he had learnt from Poe to regard as inferior, unscientific.

But other events certainly contributed, perhaps crucially, to his change of purpose—an unhappy love affair, family circumstances, the need to earn a living and a dislike for the idea of earning it in the literary market-place. The details are largely conjecture, as are the various interpretations of his 'night of crisis' in Genoa in August, 1892, when he lay on his bed while lightning flashed repeatedly into his room and "je suis entre moi et moi."[2]

What is certain is that the year 1892 marks the beginning of his 'twenty years silence' as a poet.[3] In the autumn of that year he went to Paris, found friends among the leading writers, took various jobs, wrote in prose his *Introduction a la Méthode de Léonard de Vinci* and his *Une Soirée avec M. Teste*, spent a few unhappy years as a Civil Servant, and in 1900, soon after his marriage, became secretary to Edouard Lebey, director of the Havas press agency, a post which left him plenty of time for his own preoccupations.

He studied physics and mathematics, and for many years rose at four or five every morning in order to note in a journal the workings of his own mind. He seems to have aimed at an intensified consciousness of himself; at discovering whether the operations of the pure intellect, untroubled by emotion and swept clear of irrational 'idols', were bound, like physics, by laws of their own. "The ideal aim of my thinking life seemed to me to be the attainment of such awareness of its own act and

---

[1] 'Situation de Baudelaire.' Quoted by Robert Gibson, *Modern French Poets on Poetry* (Cambridge University Press, 1961), p. 265

[2] From the symposium, *Valéry Vivant* (Cahiers du Sud, Marseilles, 1946). Quoted in *The Art of Paul Valéry*, by Francis Scarfe (Heinemann, 1954), p. 10

[3] It was not absolute, but the exceptions are unimportant

effort as to realise the condition and limits of its powers. I imagined myself as a swimmer, cut off from all that is solid, let loose in the fullness of the water and surrounded by an absence of obstacles, who thus acquires a sense of the forms and limits of his strength, from the centre of his defined powers to their furthest reach."[1]

It was not until 1912, when André Gide asked him to revise some early verses for publication, that he turned back to poetry and began to work on *La Jeune Parque*. It was published in 1917, followed three years later by *Le Cimetière Marin* and in 1922 by *Charmes*. By now he was recognised as the leading French poet of the day. Yet he continued to insist that his real interest was in the work of writing a poem, not in the finished job. Thus in commenting on *Le Cimetière Marin* he described his poetry as "an exercise rather than an action, a piece of research rather than a deliverance, a manoeuvre of myself rather than a work aimed at the public".[2]

In later life he came to allow more scope to inspiration than he had been willing to grant it at first, when he gave it credit for no more than the starting-point of a poem (*une ligne donnée*), but this was only a matter of degree. "If I had to write, I would far prefer to write something feeble in full consciousness and lucidity than to give birth in a state of trance, outside my control, to the most beautiful masterpiece."[3] Thus he refused support to the Surrealists, and they in turn attacked him, together with Poe, for approaching poetry in the manner of a 'scientific detective'—"*Crachons, en passant, sur Edgar Poe.*"[4] T. S. Eliot, in his Introduction to *The Art of Poetry*, remarks: "Valéry in fact invented, and was to impose on his age, not so much a new conception of poetry as a new conception of the poet. The tower of ivory has been fitted up as a laboratory."

[1] *A.P.*, p. 115
[2] *A.P.*, p. 116
[3] *A.P.*, p. 85. See also W. N. Ince, *The Poetic Theory of Paul Valéry* (Leicester University Press, 1961)
[4] André Breton, *Deuxième Manifeste du Surréalisme* (1930)

Yet there can be no doubt that poetry meant a great deal to Valéry, and not only while he was writing it. In his already-mentioned Preface to the *Anthologie des Poètes de la N.R.F.* he wrote: "I consider that the essence of poetry is, according to different types of mind, either quite worthless or of infinite importance; in which it is like God himself."[1] Obviously, this opinion is not quite easy to reconcile with some of his other remarks—"I don't give a damn for poetry", and so on. But we must remember that in later life he carried on a fairly steady polemic against academic conceptions of poetry in France. Thus in this same Preface he declared that "for about three hundred years the French have been taught to misunderstand the true nature of poetry and to follow, mistakenly, roads leading in a quite different direction from its home. . . . To turn a poem or to have it turned into prose, to make a poem a matter for instruction or examinations: these are no slight acts of heresy." Hence he may well have felt that by allowing himself to become an officially honoured poet, burdened with public duties, he had been drawn into a false position, associated with attitudes towards poetry that he condemned.

When in 1936 he accepted a Chair of Poetics created for him at the Collège de France, he needed the salary. He took on public functions partly, perhaps, because he wished to be viewed as a responsible citizen, not as the stereotype of a temperamental poet. But he was never quite happy in this public role, and when he broke out in protest he was, I think, saying or implying two things. First, that he had no use for the official conception of poetry. Second, that he regarded his intellectual researches as more important, more essentially part of himself, than his poetry, however highly he might value the pleasure that some poetry gave him.

He declared always that he preferred thinking to writing and wrote only to order. Yet in 1912 he returned to poetry and for the next four years was working on *La Jeune Parque*.

[1] *A.P.*, p. 85

II

Morning and Noon

SOON after the publication of *La Jeune Parque,* Valéry wrote to Mockel: "Le sujet vague de l'oeuvre est la Conscience de soi-même; la *Consciousness* de Poe, si l'on veut."[1] And the poem is in fact an interior drama of self-consciousness, of progress in self-knowledge by the Young Fate, as she explores her situation, her desires and her memories, on waking after a night of dreams. Any such progress brings knowledge not of one self but of several, more or less in conflict. That is perhaps what Valéry had felt during that 'night of crisis' in Genoa at the age of twenty-one—"je suis entre moi et moi".

There was the intellectual self, drawn to the rigorous discipline of science and mathematics, apparently the sole road to truth. There was the romantic-artistic self, in love with poetry. And a Mediterranean self, who as a boy had found rapturous pleasure in the sea and sun.[2] During his twenty years of silence as a poet, Valéry gave each self a more or less separate expression, with priority for the intellectual self. Then, in writing *La Jeune Parque,* he found a way of indirectly releasing them all; of dramatising their conflicting interplay. Not deliberately; the poem was not planned out in advance. During the four years of writing it grew and expanded, undergoing many revisions, excisions, additions. The title was not finally chosen until a few months before the poem went to press. Valéry would probably have called it *Psyche* if this title had not been already in use.

∗ ∗ ∗

Who is the Young Fate? She is first of all a young girl, waking

---

[1] *Lettres à Quelques-uns* (Gallimard, 1952)

[2] See his 'Inspirations Méditerranéennes', in *Conférences* (Editions de la N.R.F., 1939)

in the early morning, before sunrise, looking at the starry sky, hearing the threatening murmur of the sea. The night has left her troubled; the stars, 'all-powerful strangers', appear to her as accusers:

> I am alone with you at this vague time,
> Trembling, aroused from rest, and marvelling:
> What pain, I ask, has stirred my heart, what crime
> By me committed or on me performed?

She turns away from the sight of the stars; turns towards the underworld, the underworld of herself which the bite of the serpent, the destroyer of innocence, invites, and will compel, her to explore. But at first, after a passage of conflict and self-division, she rejects the serpent—

> What do you count in my eternal dream?

She turns on him with mockery; believes he can be dismissed; and the apparent dismissal of the serpent closes the first movement.

Now the Young Fate turns to memories of the time before she was aware of a divided self; when it was enough to worship the sun:

> Then, a free captive in the god's bright power,
> I trod the earth beneath his burning eye,
> Weaving my shadow through the flax in flower. . . .

But she remembers her shadow also in another guise; as the shadow-self which would never leave her—

> Between the rose and me I saw it hide
> On dance of mortal dust it fell and passed. . . .

And she realises that even in her childhood the shadow and the conflict were presaged:

> That evening which calls up a sudden flame. . . .

In this passage occurs the first allusion to the Swan-god, of whom she dreams as a saviour, but also, perhaps, as another part of herself:

The graceful throat of young Diana dreaming.

With these passages of memory a second movement seems to close.

In the next movement a central conflict emerges. Thoughts of death, as an invitation, mingle with a vision of the coming of spring, desired and yet feared:

> The air undoes me, I am pierced by cry
> Of birds like children. . . .

Her body is preparing for maternity, for giving life, but she recoils from inflicting the human condition on the shades who seem to be thronging round her, asking for this gift; yet in refusing she doubts herself, is oppressed with rising tears.

Now the motif of the sea, heard briefly at the beginning, returns; the sea beating on a rocky treacherous shore. The sea of life that could sweep her away:

> And the wind weaves, as though across a shroud,
> Confused sea-noises, waves in ruin loud. . . .
> Uncertain earth, and seaweed, carry me.

Here another movement ends.

With the opening of the next movement, the sea is calm; familiar life goes on:

> Out there, the foam is hardly to be traced,
> And always there, with every turning wave,
> The fisherman will balance in his boat.

And the offshore islands are about to catch the rising sun.

For a few moments the Young Fate is drawn back to life, but her regrets and memories return. She could still welcome death, all her attitudes are coming to seem false:

> She cannot die who in her mirror wears
> A pose of sadness, nourished by her tears.

She knows that she can neither live nor die until she has further explored herself; has made another night-journey, as though following Ariadne's thread:

> This tenuous thread whose windings blindly followed
> Have led thy life back to a morning shore. . . .

Or following the serpent, whom she now recognises as part of herself:

> Accept the serpent treasures of the deep. . . .
> (*Come down, speak low, the dark is not so dark.* . . .)

Here there is a pause, while the Young Fate sleeps. When she wakes again, it is full morning.

> Over the sea entire to where I stand
> How lovely is the spreading of the sun!
> I am still she who in thy breathing dwells,
> My veil a shadow flying towards thy land.

She goes down to the sea.

*   *   *

This brief outline—it hardly needs saying—brings one no nearer to the poem than the quotation of a few themes brings one to a symphony. ("La Jeune Parque," Valéry once said, "est d'abord et avant tout une symphonie.") The outline, too, is greatly simplified; there are complex passages and counter-themes, and difficult passages which it does not touch.

La Jeune Parque certainly is difficult; but its language and syntax are seldom obscure. It is difficult because of its swift transitions and abrupt changes of mood, and the uncertainty of what it is all 'about'. But it becomes more difficult than it need be if one expects to find it all of a piece, free from ambiguities, the logical development of a single preconceived idea.

The Young Fate herself is an ambiguous figure: a young girl, but with a suggestion of something more than human; a young girl with a real childhood, but with memories perhaps also of some kind of pre-earthly existence to which she looks back with uncertain desire. Her name, as Mr. Francis Scarfe has pointed out,[1] has associations with the Parcae, the Roman goddesses who presided over birth, the entry into life. Or one can take her two natures to represent a conflict in Valéry himself . . . but no such interpretation will be entirely right, nor will it be important.

Whatever one finds in *La Jeune Parque*—its complexities, apparent contradictions, confusing time-sequences and contrasting planes of consciousness—are there for one chief reason only: they enabled Valéry to write the kind of poetry he wanted to write. "Literature," he once said, "interests me *profoundly* only to the extent to which it urges the mind to certain transformations—those in which the stimulating properties of language play the chief part. . . . The force to bend the common word to unexpected ends without violating the 'time-honoured forms', the capture and subjection of things that are difficult to say, and above all the simultaneous management of syntax, harmony and ideas (which is the problem of the purest poetry) are in my eyes the supreme objects of our art."[2]

"Things that are difficult to say"—or (one might add) actually impossible to say except in poetry. "It seems clear," Professor D. W. Harding remarks, "that a writer, especially a poet, using words, images and incidents with evaluative or symbolic overtones, is likely very often to convey meanings which he can't be said to have intended before writing and which he may not observe even when he reads over what he has written."[3] But how can a metrical pattern 'say' more than a prose pattern? And what are the things that only poetry can say? These are obviously basic questions; we shall come to them. Here I will add only that poetry has two voices, inextricably mingled: its own distinctive voice, and a prose voice, or prose meaning, which it cannot do without. If poetry tries to get right away from prose meaning, to include *nothing* that can be paraphrased,

[1] *The Art of Paul Valéry,* op. cit.
[2] *A.P.,* p. 145
[3] *Experience into Words* (Chatto and Windus, 1963), p. 185

it will limit itself to communicating, at best, a very small range of tenuous experience. It becomes a fragile or exotic flower, with no roots in human soil. Valéry (we shall see) toyed with this aspiration towards 'pure poetry'; it attracted him; but he was too intellectual a poet to hold to it for long, and too intelligent to suppose that it ever could be completely realised.

*   *   *

The underlying theme of *Le Cimetière Marin*—the polarity between the eternal, the absolute, and the realm of human life—is essentially the same as in *La Jeune Parque*, but transposed now into a quieter key, and objectified. Instead of an interior drama we have an external landscape, a cemetery on a hillside over-looking the Mediterranean; the scene of Valéry's boyhood. The sun burns overhead; the sea is calm. White sails are moving on it.

The voice now is Valéry's own; he meditates on life and death. And in the various aspects of the scene the conflicting course of his meditations is reflected. Above is the clear, brilliant sky, the absolute, the realm of pure thought:

> High noon above, noon standing motionless—

Below is the sea; the sea in which as a boy he had bathed with passionate pleasure. Around him are the emblems and monuments of death—

> Marbles trembling under veils of shade—

where the pleasure of thought and the pleasures of living will both be finally subsumed.

Religious consolations are rejected—the 'useless dream'. And the pleasures of pure thinking lead—where? The realm of the absolute, eternally self-sufficient, is indifferent to man:

> The careless serene brilliance seems to sow
> Over the height its sovereign disdain. . . .

All meditations, reflections, are in the end vain, as Zeno's paradoxes imply. The conclusion recalls the ending of *La Jeune Parque*. The wind rises; the sea crashes on the rocks.

> Awake, my body, break this cast of thought—

The poet turns to the sea, the ever-youthful, life-renewing sea.

*　　*　　*

Of course, there is much more in *Le Cimetière Marin* than that, and it is the more that matters; not the framework, nor any interpretation. Valéry treated the various interpreters of his poems very kindly, but he always insisted that *"there is no true meaning to a text*—no author's authority. Whatever he may have *wanted to say*, he has written what he has written. Once published, a text is like an apparatus that anyone may use as he will and according to his ability: it is not certain that the one who constructed it can use it better than another."[1]

[1] *A.P.*, p. 152

III

The Condition of Music

LATE in life, Valéry wrote a Preface for a new edition of a translation into French verse, made in 1641 by Father Cyprian, a Carmelite monk, of the *Spiritual Canticles* of St. John of the Cross. Mysticism was for Valéry (he says) a foreign field, but this did not impair his response to Father Cyprian's translation. He praises it warmly for its extraordinary success in closely following the Spanish and yet turning it into a poetry which 'sings'. And he adds, characteristically, "There is no other test of poetry."[1]

Similarly, Valéry would not have thought it mattered whether a reader of *Le Cimetière Marin* agreed with its non-religious ideas. The poem was not written to expound ideas; they were the themes for its music. The first impulse towards it sprang, he tells us, from "a rhythmic figure, empty, or filled with meaningless syllables, which obsessed me for some time"— a rhythm of ten syllables to a line. Gradually the rhythm drew to itself the memories and images and reflections with which the poem was composed.

Composed—for with Valéry the writing of poetry was not very unlike the writing of music. He was of course not aiming merely at melodious verbal effects, he wished his poetry to have something of the expressive character of music, which conveys

---

[1] *A.P.*, p. 285. As an example of Father Cyprian's style, here is his rendering of the opening of the *Canticles*:

> A l'ombre d'une obscure Nuict
> D'angoisseux amour embrasée
> O l'heureux sort qui me conduit,
> Je sortis sans estre avisée
> Le calme tenant à propos
> Ma maison en un doux repos. . . .

an experience indefinable in any other terms. Thus of some lines in *Fragments de Narcisse* he wrote: "Observe that they are entirely devoid of ideas and thus attain that degree of purity which properly constitutes what I call pure poetry."[1]

A strange attitude, this might seem, in so intellectual a poet, for ideas, rather than sentiments or human relations, were Valéry's absorbing interest; his poetry is woven out of them. But he would have liked the ideas to be completely dissolved in the poetry, so that they could not be detached and discussed on their own account; for that, he believed, would interfere with the particular experience or state of mind which he wanted poetry to induce.

Here one must recall the opening words of his early essay, written after his first discovery of Poe: "Literature is the art of playing on the minds of others." He never moved far from this view; in a lecture at Oxford in 1939, six years before his death, he made it more explicit: "A poem is really a kind of machine for producing the poetic state by means of words."[2]

He made various attempts to describe the 'poetic state'; the following, from his *Pure Poetry: Notes for a Lecture*, is one of the clearest:

> As for independent poetic emotion, we must note that it is distinguished from other human emotions by a unique characteristic, an admirable property: it tends to give us the feeling of an illusion or the illusion of a world (a *world* in which events, images, beings and things, although resembling those which people the ordinary world, are in an inexplicable but intimate

---

[1] Quoted by Gibson, op. cit., p. 123. When the Abbé Brémond took up the phrase, 'pure poetry', as evidence for his thesis that poetry leads towards a form of mystical experience, Valéry replied (*Cours de Poétique*, Lecture 11): "I have never taken this term 'pure' in any other sense than that used by chemists. I was asking myself whether it might be possible to single out, in the course of writing, the specifically poetic elements and to compose a work of them alone. My friend Brémond saw in the word 'pure' a mystical notion: that was not my intention." See also Henri Brémond, *Prayer and Poetry*; trans. Algar Thorold (Burns Oates and Washbourne, 1927)

[2] 'Poetry and Abstract Thought', *A.P.*

relationship with the whole of our sensibility). Known objects and beings are in a way—if I may be forgiven the expression—*musicalised*; they have become resonant to each other and as though tuned to our sensibility. Thus defined, the poetic world has great affinities with the state of dreaming, at least with the state produced in certain dreams.[1]

Valéry never tried to explain how the 'poetic state' arose or what it signified. He recorded it as fact of experience, but to explain it was a task for a science of the future. "If one knew a little more about it, one could hope in consequence to form a fairly clear idea of the poetic essence. But we are far from possessing this central science. . . . Everything in this field of research must be created—and not only the means, the methods, the terms and the notions—but also, and above all, the very object of our curiosity must be defined."[2] He was temperamentally unable to read into the 'poetic state' any transcendental significance, as most of the Symbolists had done. Thus he was compelled to leave the poetry he most valued, the poetry that approaches the condition of music, open to the charge that it provides merely a dreamlike pleasure for a minority of aesthetes and has nothing important to 'say'. Eliot, in his Introduction to *The Art of Poetry*, touches on this:

> The one complaint which I am tempted to make against Valéry's poetics is that it provides us with no criterion of seriousness. He is deeply concerned with the problem of process, of how the poem is made, but not with the question of how it is related to the rest of life in such a way as to give the reader the shock of feeling that the poem has been to him, not merely an experience, but a serious experience.

Eliot is of course speaking here of Valéry's poetics, not of his poetry, and as a poet Valéry was fortunately not able to follow strictly his own professed view of what 'pure poetry' should be. He regarded the ideas in his poetry as incidental, but his poetry

[1] *A.P.*, p. 187. A similar passage occurs in Valéry's Oxford lecture.
[2] *A.P.*, p. 7

gains from them an intellectual fibre which protects it from degenerating into a near-meaningless music. Moreover, although he did not write *La Jeune Parque* or *Le Cimetière Marin* in order to debate any particular human issues, they are there . . . between the eternal light of reason and the shadow of mortality, how should we choose to live? The issues are not discussed in abstract terms, but in those of imagery and recollection; lifted out of their context they become as lustreless as a shell may do when taken from the sea. But the imagery springs from them, and through the imagery they are experienced.

In his poetics, however, Valéry is so often bent on showing, in face of the French academic tradition, what poetry is not—i.e. not merely a means of embodying ideas or reflections or descriptions in a metrical form—that he seems to take a restrictive view of what poetry can accomplish and of how many different kinds of good poetry there can be. Poetry, he says, must 'sing', and it must create the 'poetic state'. The first requirement would rule out a great deal of poetry which does not sing in any obvious sense but yet has verbal potency. As to the second requirement, I think Valéry was right in principle, for unless a poem (and the same applies to any work of art) is operative—unless it acts on and changes the reader's consciousness—it will lack the distinctive power and virtue of poetry and should perhaps go by another name. In a long poem this will not happen all the time (hence Poe's remark that there are no long poems), but it should happen often enough to keep the reader aware of being in the presence of poetry. The well-known aphorism, "A poem should not mean but be", seems to me misleading, unless taken merely as a warning against supposing that the discursive meaning of a poem is its sole important content. A poem should not be but do; and its doing is indispensable for transmitting some of its meanings.

More generally, one might say, Art is what art does. For in this realm good intentions, lofty aims, even hard work and expert technique, count for nothing in themselves; the final operative effect, which is also the transmitter of meanings, is what matters. This is not a criterion of rank; the all-round merit of a work of art depends on the range and depth of the meanings it transmits. But unless it has an operative effect, it will transmit only a prosaic meaning.

I am well aware that there is no general agreement on some of these points; they open up an old battlefield where actions are still going on. The very existence of a distinctive 'poetic state', or 'aesthetic state', has been denied; or, if not absolutely denied, condemned as a self-indulgent escapism, irrelevant to the real purpose and value of works of art.

I think the immediate motive of these attacks has often been a dislike of something apparently irrational, something that seems to border on the magical or mystical and cannot be scientifically explained. But the attacks are justified, up to a point, if the 'poetic state' is treated simply as an exquisite state of mind which, once it has been induced, can be savoured for its own sake, irrespective of any contribution it might make to a better understanding of the poem. On this basis, all poems which induced the poetic state would be of equal merit. Nobody, perhaps, has ever taken exactly that view of the poetic state, but a tendency towards it does run through a certain aesthetic tradition which in this country stems chiefly from Pater and his disciples. It leads away from intercourse with the substance of a poem towards using the poem for a kind of mental masturbation.

But the fact that the poetic state can be abused does not mean that we can do without it. Nothing else will open the door to an apprehension of all the meanings of a poem, the ordinary discursive and the multiple symbolical.

But what is the poetic state? What kinds of meaning does it transmit? As a scientifically-minded intellectual, Valéry could find no satisfactory answers to these troublesome questions, and therefore no satisfying grounds for valuing poetry as more than a private pleasure.

These questions remain: we shall try to go a little further into them. I have started with Valéry because in him the central difficulty is illustrated as a fact of experience. Poetry speaks with two voices, but for the pure intellect—Valéry's Monsieur Teste—the symbolic voice is meaningless, an irritating distraction which overlays the ordinary meaning with pretentious ornament.

When a poet and a scientifically-inclined thinker are united in one man, their marriage will not be easy. In Valéry the 'two cultures' met, and almost sterilised each other.

This is the conflict that arose on a broader scale in Europe when nineteenth-century science clashed with the Romantic movement; later it became a central issue for the Symbolists. But before coming to this, we must be clear what we are going to mean by 'symbol' and 'image'.

IV

Symbols and Signs

PERHAPS the best way of delimiting a symbol is to distinguish
it from a sign. When Ophelia says, "There is pansies, that's
for thoughts", the pansies are a sign. They point away from
themselves to something they stand for. If Ophelia were to say
only "There is pansies", the phrase would have no significance
unless we already knew that pansies stand for thoughts in the
conventional 'language of flowers'.

When Blake writes:

> Ah, Sun-flower! weary of time,
> Who countest the steps of the Sun,
> Seeking after that sweet golden clime
> Where the traveller's journey is done. . . .

we cannot say exactly what the sunflower stands for. We are
not pointed away from it towards something else; we enter into
an experience of which the sunflower is a part.

The same word can, of course, serve as a sign in one context
and as a symbol in another. If I say, "Pass the salt", the word
'salt' is a sign, serving merely to designate the substance I want.
But in "Ye are the salt of the earth", the word is a symbol,
charged with various meanings and associations.

Thus a symbol, unlike a sign, will always have several
meanings. We can choose to focus attention on one, but the
others will still be there, active in the half-conscious background.

A sign, again, is replaceable by any intelligible equivalent; a
symbol is not. "Pass the sodium chloride" means the same as
"Pass the salt". But "Ye are the sodium chloride of the earth"—
the literal meaning is the same, but the symbolic potency has
vanished.[1]

[1] This distinction between 'symbols' and 'signs' is the one developed by

An allegory is an elaborated form of sign. An extended allegory may include symbolic passages, but allegory is useful mainly for teaching—for the pictorial exposition of ideas—not for directly communicating experience. "An allegory," Coleridge says, "is but a translation of abstract notions into a picture-language, which is itself nothing but an abstraction from objects of the senses. . . . On the other hand a symbol is characterised by a translucence of the special in the individual, or of the general in the special, or of the universal in the general; above all by the translucence of the eternal through and in the temporal."[1] Goethe put it more briefly: "In a true symbol the particular represents the universal, not as a dream or shadow, but as the living and instantaneous revelation of the unfathomable."

A verbal image in its simplest form is a picture called up before the mental eye. If a phrase in poetry does no more than that, it is a sign, pointing to the scene it describes. It may be an agreeably melodious sign, calling up a vivid picture:

> The stag at eve had drunk his fill
> Where danced the moon on Monan's rill. . . .

But the language remains descriptive. When Meredith writes:

> Darker grows the valley, more and more forgetting

the image is symbolic; it calls up a scene, but also communicates an experience of which the darkening valley is a part.

Verbal images, therefore, are of service to poetry in two

Susanne Langer in her *Philosophy in a New Key* (1942). In her later books she follows Charles W. Morris (see her *Feeling and Form*, p. 26n) in using 'sign' as a generic term to cover 'symbols' and 'signals', now taking 'signals' to mean what she had previously meant by 'signs'. I find it clearer to distinguish between 'signs' and 'symbols' and to treat 'signals'—normally associated with action—as a special class of 'signs'.

[1] From 'The Statesman's Manual', *Complete Works of Samuel Taylor Coleridge* (Harper and Brothers, New York, 1884); volume one, p. 437

distinct but overlapping ways: for descriptive purposes and as symbols. But poetry does not depend on them:

> If thou didst ever hold me in thy heart,
> Absent thee from felicity a while,
> And in this harsh world draw thy breath in pain,
> To tell my story.

These lines do not (for me) call up an image; their effect—aided in some indefinable but essential way by the sounds of the words—is to make the reader participate in the experience that will be Horatio's after Hamlet's death, and at the same time to participate in the darkening atmosphere that is falling over the close of the play. They do not correspond exactly to Aristotle's definition of metaphor as "the intuitive perception of the similarity in dissimilars", but they are metaphorical in so far as some phrases ("hold me in thy heart . . . draw thy breath in pain") are not to be read literally. They could be taken to illustrate Eliot's 'objective correlative', a kind of metaphor: "The only way of expressing emotion in the form of art is by finding an 'objective correlative'; in other words, a set of objects, a situation, a chain of events which shall be the formula of that *particular* emotion; such that when the external facts, which must terminate in sensory experience, are given, the emotion is immediately invoked."[1]

Poetry has constantly to make use of metaphorical language in order to communicate feelings and intuitive perceptions that cannot be directly described—so much so that "it would be hard, perhaps impossible," Mr. Donald Davie observes, "to find a poem in English where the literal statement is completely unmetaphorical".[2] Hence there is something in Aristotle's celebrated dictum that "the greatest thing of all by far is to be a master of metaphor. It is the one thing that cannot be learnt from others, and it is also a sign of original genius." But his

[1] From 'Hamlet', 1919; reprinted in Eliot's *Selected Essays, 1917–1932* (Faber, 1932), p. 145
[2] *Purity of Diction in English Verse* (Chatto and Windus, 1952), p. 31

definition of metaphor seems to me too rigid, as any such brief definition is likely to be; for if we try to establish exact distinctions between metaphor, symbol and image, we find them merging into one another, and I would rather distinguish them in terms of their effects. A poetic symbol is recognised by its power to act on the reader's consciousness and make him participate in the otherwise indefinable experience which it communicates. Metaphors and images are often symbolic, but not always; it depends on their quality and on how and why they are used.

In the modern history of poetry, however, the 'doctrine of the image' (derived through the Imagists from Symbolism) has a special place, for in the early twenties it promoted the revolutionary new style which allowed a poem to be composed largely out of images, often strung together with no obvious logical links:

> The circles of the stormy moon
> Slide westward toward the River Plate,
> Death and the Raven drift above
> And Sweeney guards the hornèd gate.

Thus the 'doctrine of the image' has some connection with the ideal of 'pure poetry'—a poetry which would consist entirely of images, with all discursive language eliminated. Any such poems are bound to be brief and limited; Imagism was a short-lived movement. But the doctrine of the image has been fruitful in extending the scope of modern poetry by liberating it from the requirements of ordinary syntax and logical sequence. It has also been harmful in licensing private obscurity; but in these developments the bad has to be taken with the good. The good does not redeem the bad; neither does the bad incriminate the good.

Symbolic potency, however, is found also in prose. So we come to the familiar question: How can poetry be distinguished, except formally, from prose? Can we draw a line and say that everything on one side of it is poetry and everything on the other side is prose?

I think we can, on one condition: we must be content with a subjective test, not giving exactly the same result for everyone. Poetry can be individually recognised when it brings about a sort of illuminated perception of the poem's symbolic meanings; whatever the poem is speaking of appears in a transfigured light. Thus it induces in the reader the 'poetic state'.

One reason why formal poetry has this effect is that straightforward prose has an irregular rhythm while formal poetry has a recurrent rhythm, or at least a recurrent beat, sometimes fortified by another type of recurrence, rhyme. This recurrent beat tends to lull the surface consciousness and to open freer access for the words to reach and stir the unconscious. Hence it is that images and turns of phrase which would be out of place in prose are acceptable in poetry; the unconscious will accept and respond to a great deal that the conscious mind cannot assimilate.

Yeats makes a similar point (allowing for the rather curious phraseology of an early essay): "The purpose of rhythm, it has always seemed to me, is to prolong the moment of contemplation, the moment when we are both asleep and awake, which is the one moment of creation, by hushing us with an alluring monotony, while it holds us waking by variety, to keep us in that state of perhaps real trance, in which the mind liberated from the pressure of the will is unfolded in symbols."[1]

Another way of putting the distinction between poetry and prose is to repeat that straightforward prose has a single, discursive meaning, while good poetry has several meanings—a discursive or referential meaning and a range of symbolic meanings—and its symbolic meanings are not experienced unless the reader's consciousness is changed. The discursive meaning can be paraphrased in prose; the symbolic meanings cannot. The nearer poetry gets to lyrical song, the further it moves away from prose into a territory of its own.

After making these distinctions, however, we find that

[1] From 'The Symbolism of Poetry', 1900; reprinted in *Essays and Introductions* (Macmillan, 1961), p. 159

although they are satisfactory in placing all good formal verse on one side of the line and a very high percentage of prose on the other, we are left with two special forms of prose—prose which remains prose and yet has a poetic effect, and that unpleasant hybrid, 'prose-poetry', which tries to produce poetic effects but fails to achieve them. Why does it fail?

Perhaps the main reason is that prose-poetry promises a symbolic meaning which is not present, or only vaguely suggested, not embodied in the words, many of which are mere emotive trimming. The reader's mind is stirred a little and then immediately frustrated; nothing clearly discernible on the symbolic level is there. At the same time the discursive meaning is often blurred by the verbiage, and it too may fail to come through clearly.

One might then ask how any prose can have genuine poetic effects, without the aid of a formal verse structure. Perhaps all one can say is that it does; this is a fact of experience. It lacks the recurrent beat of verse, but it has a rhythm of its own, and it uses images and verbal associations and resonances to act on the consciousness in the same way. Or perhaps not in exactly the same way, but near enough.

The range of good poetic prose is limited: it seems best suited to eloquent and stately or elegiac effects. Familiar examples could be drawn from the Authorised Version of the Bible, starting with the first chapter of Genesis: "And the earth was without form, and void; and darkness was upon the face of the deep. And the Spirit of God moved upon the face of the waters. And God said, Let there be light; and there was light."

For an example in a very different modern style, one I remember is the opening of Hemingway's novel, *A Farewell to Arms*:[1]

In the late summer of that year we lived in a house in a village that looked across the river and the plain to the mountains.

[1] Cape, 1929

In the bed of the river there were pebbles and boulders, dry and white in the sun, and the water was clear and swiftly moving and blue in the channels. Troops went by the house and down the road and the dust they raised powdered the leaves of the trees. The trunks of the trees too were dusty and the leaves fell early that year and we saw the troops marching along the road and the dust rising and leaves, stirred by the breeze, falling and the soldiers marching and afterwards the road bare and white except for the leaves.

Examples of prose-poetry would not be hard to find: the field ranges from occasional passages in the works of some famous writers down through romantic magazine stories to advertising copy of the lusher kind. But it would be invidious, I feel, to pick a single example from some eminent source, and there is little need perhaps for any examples. Prose-poetry is less common nowadays than it used to be; it may be a dying art, or vice. It can be recognised by a few constant traits, giving an impression of inflation, of forcing the note, of asking the words to carry more emotional traffic than they will bear.

If we are going so discuss the future of poetry in an age of science, we can leave all variants of prose aside and limit ourselves to recognisable verse. Poetic prose seldom stands by itself; generally it occurs in the midst of straightforward prose writing. Hence it is much less exposed than formal verse to the "What is the use of it?" kind of question. Not declaring itself to be poetry, it is less likely to be held up and searched.

★   ★   ★

Now, having cleared the ground a little, we can return to the question of what poetry 'says'. What does it give to the reader, through its heightening action on consciousness, that ordinary prose cannot give?

One answer (going back at least to Neoplatonism in the West and much farther back in the East) is the transcendental: poetry opens the door to some superior realm of being which lies behind the phenomenal world and transcends it.

The danger of any transcendental aesthetic is that it may seem to reduce poetry (and the other arts) to a means of experiencing something *else*. Why then resort to works of art as door-openers: is there not some more direct and penetrating way of access to this higher realm?

But this is to misunderstand what poetry does. It does not give experience of a transcendent realm, separate from the phenomenal world. A poem must have *some* discursive mean-ing—i.e. it must be about something in the phenomenal world. When the poem is experienced, this subject-matter does not disappear, to make way for a higher vision. It is still there, but in some way changed, transfused, illuminated; and not alone, but in relation to its context.

What then is the subject transfused by? The answer generally given in modern times, and particularly since the beginning of the Romantic movement, is that it is transfused by the poet's feelings about it. He has experienced the subject in a special way, not by observing it from outside but by merging his feelings with it. The poem's function is to communicate, through images and symbols and other special uses of words, the poet's response to the world—his experience of it and the feelings this arouses in him. According to this theory, therefore, if the world appears to be transfused or transformed under the influence of poetry, this is in one sense an illusion. The poetry is not revealing any-thing that belongs intrinsically to the world; it is giving expres-sion to what the poet feels about it.

This may be called the expression theory of poetry, as distinct from the transcendental theory, according to which a poem does not *only* communicate the poet's response to the world but enables the reader to apprehend some true but normally hidden aspect of the world itself.

Here I am simply stating the two theories briefly. Later I shall explore them further and try to show that they are not finally incompatible. But they have often been treated as rivals and they have different historical roots. I believe they need to be understood in relation to the evolution of consciousness. Having discussed this in a previous book,[1] I will mention here only a few brief points.

The normal consciousness today is an onlooker-consciousness; we stand away from nature and view it as something quite apart from ourselves. But this is a recent phase; not very long ago men still had a participating consciousness: they entered into the world of nature and enjoyed a communicative experience with it that we have mostly lost. In still earlier times they had also an awareness of an active spiritual background from which nature was sustained; that is the basis of mythology. It was only when this awareness came to be lost that they felt free to treat nature as an inert body, so to speak, and to dissect it experimentally.

This new attitude marks the onset in Europe, during the 15th century, of the onlooker-consciousness, a transition reflected in many fields, including the practice and interpretation of the arts. Until then, a transcendental view of art had generally been held, or something like it had been taken for granted. Early art is thus mostly in the service of religion. It is not realist in the sense of seeking to reproduce accurately the external world, nor is it concerned with exploring the inner world of the artist.

The Greeks, precocious in so many ways, did tend towards artistic realism. Thus Plato was led to banish poets from his ideal State because (he believed) they drew attention away from the realm of archetypal ideas to the inferior realm of fictitious copies. But a transcendental view of art has always prevailed (often one-sidedly) in the East, and was reintroduced in the West by Plotinus. In Renaissance Italy it flourished for the last time.

Realism in painting (bound up with the discovery of perspective early in the 15th century) is one of the first symptoms of the onlooker-age. Soon afterwards a new interest in introspection shows itself; Hamlet appears. The onlooker, standing self-consciously apart from the world, has two distinct fields of interest—the world and himself. "Enough here to remark that

[1] *Towards a Third Culture* (Faber, 1961)

40

the isolation of the world from the self—the method of the physical sciences—and the isolation of the self from the world—the method of introspective biography and romantic poetry—are complementary phases of a single process."[1]

Here I must pause to emphasise that the emergence of the onlooker-consciousness is not something to be deplored. It gives men a new capacity for clear objective thinking and exact experiment; without it we should not have had modern science. And the dangers of some features of scientific progress, familiar today, should not obscure the equally evident fact that without modern science men would have remained prisoners of their environment, a prey to incomprehensible diseases and famines, with no way out from chronic poverty for the multititude. It is human destiny to explore deeply the material world, and to learn painfully how to control the hazards of this modern enterprise.

But there is loss as well as gain. The focus of consciousness narrows, giving a sharper picture of the world, necessary for scientific investigation, but there is a corresponding loss of that wider, participating awareness which gave meaning to the picture. The gains are generally recognised, but the loss is not. Yet I think it is essential to reckon in the loss if the change from a mediaeval to a modern outlook, and its influence on the arts, are to be understood. "Steeped as our age is in the ideas of evolution, we have not yet become accustomed to the idea that consciousness itself is something that has evolved through long centuries and that even today, with us, it is still evolving. . . . But of course the concept of evolution cannot here be interpreted in the simple and unilinear fashion of nineteenth-century thought, as in Hegel and Spencer, but rather in its full concreteness and ambiguity, as simultaneously gain and loss, advance and regress."[2]

The onlooker acquires a new impulse to explore the outer

[1] Lewis Mumford, *Technics and Civilisation* (Routledge, 1934), p. 130
[2] William Barrett, *Irrational Man: a Study in Existential Philosophy* (Heinemann, 1961), p. 72

world, geographically and scientifically, but he no longer finds in his own experience any grounds for supposing that the world has anything 'behind' it, any transcendental dimension for the arts to reveal. Hence for the artist there remain, at first, two possibilities—he can portray the outer world 'just as it is', or looks to be in true perspective, or he can turn to his inner life and give expression to that. Realism in the graphic arts goes together with the beginnings of subjective literature. This polarity is reflected in the conflict that presently arose between the scientific outlook and the Romantic movement.

V

Romantic Feeling

POETRY in the 18th century came under the influence of the rational virtues which the prestige of Newtonian science had brought into vogue. "The choice of the heroic couplet as the dominant form", Sir Ifor Evans observes, "arose from a desire for a medium that was ordered, precise, and employable in analysis and criticism. It is difficult at any later stage to discover such a parallel influence from science upon literature, affecting not only ideas but the very structure of verse."[1]

Besides this more or less direct influence, the new scientific outlook helped to establish a cool social climate which was reflected back into poetry. "The proper form for the matter of poets in the Augustan tradition may fairly be said to have the virtues of good prose. In that tradition the poet inhabited, not

The place of solitude where three dreams cross,

but (even when solitary) the social world—the world of common sense waking consciousness. His matter, even when contemplated privately, and with strong personal feelings, always found it natural to acknowledge the jurisdiction of reason. Each word in his verse knows how it got there, and can give a neat and satisfactory account of its presence; we talk of 'propriety' and 'precision'—'conscious neatness and precision of statement'. Even the formal pattern of the verse, suggesting as it does a critical sobriety and a steady deference to rational order, might be said to express a prose attitude of mind: it certainly has a great deal to do with the effect of prose voice making prose statements."[2]

[1] *Literature and Science* (Allen and Unwin, 1954), p. 23
[2] F. R. Leavis, *Revaluation* (Chatto and Windus, 1936), p. 123

43

The Romantic movement was primarily a protest against the deadening conventions which had hardened round this rational style; but quite other energies soon flowed into it. The Romantic poets were hardly at all influenced by William Blake, then little known or understood, but Blake, with his insistence that the outlook promoted by Newtonian science was a darkening of the imagination, a kind of sleep, had said explicitly what most of the Romantic poets came to feel. Shelley, it is true, looked forward with excited hope to the scientific future, when steam boats would ply on Lac Léman; but Keats's anxieties were more representative of the coming trend. In his *Lamia* occurs the familiar passage (where 'philosophy', of course, means natural philosophy, or what we should call science):

> Do not all charms fly
> At the mere touch of cold philosophy?
> There was an awful rainbow once in heaven:
> We know her woof, her texture; she is given
> In the dull catalogue of common things.
> Philosophy will clip an Angel's wings,
> Conquer all mysteries by rule and line,
> Empty the haunted air and gnomed mine—
> Unweave a rainbow, as it erewhile made
> The tender-personed Lamia melt into a shade.

Similar fears were heard at intervals during the 19th century, but Keats is sufficiently relevant.[1] In these lines from *Lamia* there may be several anxieties mingled, but they are all connected with a fear that science will rob nature of 'mysteries'. The Romantics liked mysteries of most kinds, and not only in the superficial sense of a detective story or a ghost story. As long as an object or an idea retains some mystery, it can suggest various meanings; in other words it may have a symbolic character which appeals to the unconscious as well as to the conscious mind.

[1] For other examples see M. H. Abrams, *The Mirror and the Lamp* (New York: Oxford University Press, 1953), Chapter XI

Science cannot like mysteries; its task is to explain them, up to a point. With the 'awful rainbow', this point is reached when the meteorological conditions favourable to the appearance of rainbows are understood, and when rainbows can be produced artificially, at least on a laboratory scale. But why, given these physical conditions, we should perceive the rainbow not as a set of wave-lengths, and not as a series of nerve impulses in the brain, but as a multi-coloured arch out there in the sky—this remains a mystery which for practical purposes science does not need to solve, even if it could be solved in scientific terms, which seems doubtful. And this mystery of the rainbow is of course only one small part of the general mystery of the phenomenal world—how it comes to be there at all, with its prodigious variety of forms and colours, and how we come to perceive it. Our perceptions of it are connected somehow with light signals and nerve currents, but a scientific account of these leaves untouched the outer scene that we actually perceive: nor need it impoverish our awareness of it—unless anyone who sees a rainbow translates it immediately into wave-lengths and so on, and then assumes (with no warrant) that the wave-lengths are more 'real' than the rainbow itself.

But these elementary considerations are not enough to dispose of Keats's anxieties. The advent of modern science *is* relevant to the seeing of rainbows, for it reflects a change in the norm of human consciousness, and seeing as an experience depends on the level of consciousness from which it proceeds. For most people today, visual experience of the world is not likely to be quite the same as it was when human consciousness was still naturally capable of entering with participation into the outer scene, instead of merely observing it—'onlooking' it—from outside.

This detached 'onlooking' is necessary at times for a scientist, but it is not very congenial to most poets. A poet generally wishes to enter with his feelings into the outer world and to find there something to which his feelings can respond. Or one might say that he wishes to discern in the world some phrases of that symbolic language which is also the language of poetry. Keats seems to have feared chiefly that 'cold philosophy' would undermine this kind of experience by presenting it as an illusion to which no sensible man should succumb. He may also have had some intimation that in the onlooker-age such experiences would actually become less accessible.

How this can happen was very clearly exemplified, a little later in the 19th century, by Wordsworth, who both recorded it in his poetry and painfully went through it in the course of his own life:

> There was a time when meadow, grove, and stream,
> The earth, and every common sight,
>   To me did seem
>   Apparelled in celestial light,
> The glory and the freshness of a dream
> It is not now as it hath been of yore;—
>   Turn whereso'er I may,
>   By night or day,
> The things which I have seen I now can see no more.

Wordsworth experienced with rare intensity the transition from a participating mode of consciousness to the onlooker mode.

But Keats need not have feared that poetry would die. Wordsworth's fate is not inevitable for poets, nor is the loss of participation a final phase. Something like participation still comes naturally to most young children, and in it are the seeds of that outgoing imagination, that power of entering with imaginative sympathy into other lives and modes of being, which we should look on as promising a renewal of participation in a more conscious form. In a child who survives the ordeal of education, the seeds may flower—perhaps in poetry, or in some other art, or perhaps in an approach to nature which is neither sentimental nor coldly analytical.

Moreover, if an imaginative capacity is present in adult life, poetry can be written out of almost any mood, including those moods of doubt and pessimism which are characteristic of the onlooker-age. Certain kinds of poetry become difficult or impossible to write, and poetry itself tends to become more difficult, less simple and spontaneous; but anything that human beings feel and experience with some intensity *can* be a source of poetry.

The questions that do arise in the onlooker-age are concerned not so much with the writing of poetry as with the audience for it—will it continue to be valued and at all widely read? The other arts all have some social function which at least keeps them going: they are needed for decoration or ceremonial or entertainment. Poetry has no such claim on public support; and (as Valéry felt) a good scientific reason for valuing it, except as a quite private pleasure for the few, is not easy to find. During the 19th century poetry was in fact attacked quite explicitly on this ground by exponents of the new Utilitarian rationalism. They argued, in effect, that there is no need for poetry, since anything worth saying can be said more soberly and truthfully in prose. "Between poetry and truth", Bentham declared firmly, "there is a natural opposition. . . . The poet always stands in need of something false. When he pretends to lay his foundations in truth, the ornaments of his structure are fictions; his business consists in stimulating our passions, and exciting our prejudices. Truth, exactitude of every kind, is fatal to poetry."[1]

What sort of answers would have been relevant to this line of attack? The need is to show that poetry reveals forms of truth which are outside the range of scientific discourse. These truths could have to do with the world, or with the inner life of human beings, or perhaps with both at once. But to say that poetry reveals hidden truths about the world is to go a long way towards a transcendental theory of poetry, and the English Romantics hardly ever took this step; Blake had no immediate heirs. Coleridge was temperamentally inclined towards a transcendental aesthetic, and at times, under the

[1] From *The Rationale of Rewards and Punishments*, 1825. A similar attitude was taken by Peacock (though perhaps rather less seriously), and later, with some variations, by Taine in France

congenial influence of Schelling and other German Romantic philosophers, he came very near it, but in other places he draws back, as though anxious not to claim for art any function proper to religion.[1] In the letters of Keats there are well-known passages on imagination which may seem to point towards a transcendental aesthetic, but Keats did not live to work them out. The Romantics mostly left it to religion to dispute with science about the nature of the world. They believed that imagination could illuminate the world, but only in so far as the world was transfused by the poet's feelings. Hence for the truth in poetry they looked inward; here in the inner life were the truths that poetry, but not science, could communicate.

This was a partial answer to the rationalist critics, and it is in fact the answer that has generally been given in various more sophisticated forms (as we shall see) ever since. In no form does it seem to me quite satisfactory, but in its original Romantic form it was not only inadequate, but misleading; and it had unfortunate results. The most familiar indication of this is Wordsworth's "All good poetry is the spontaneous overflow of powerful feelings"—a perilous definition only slightly qualified (in the same Preface to *Lyrical Ballads*) by the remark that poetry "takes its origin from emotion recollected in tranquillity".

Obviously there is some truth in this; good poetry is never written unless some feeling goes into it; nor is it ever experienced without some response of feeling in the reader. But the definition is perilous because of the encouragement it gives to the idea that anyone who lets strong feelings flow out into verse is writing poetry. It also encourages the idea that a poet's business is specially to cultivate his emotions, even to a lachry-

---

[1] "Coleridge does not make any special cognitive claims for poetry. In his philosophy, it is specifically the reason, not the secondary imagination, which is the 'organ of the supersensuous', with 'the power of acquainting itself with invisible realities or spiritual objects', with the result that religion and poetry remain distinct." M. H. Abrams, *The Mirror and the Lamp*, op. cit., p. 314

mose degree, and that these personal emotions are what he has somehow to transmit to the reader. And the Wordsworthian expression theory has in fact led to a vast amount of feeble versification, evident not only in minor journals but in some of the later pages of the *Golden Treasury* and the *Oxford Book of English Verse*.

*   *   *

In this cultivation of an inner realm of feeling, as the only place where the truths of poetry did not have to meet the competition of the truths asserted by science, we can see both a frustration of the original hopes of the Romantic movement and the beginning of that rift between science and the arts which has led to the 'two cultures' controversy of our own time. The young Romantics had greeted the French Revolution as heralding a new age of freedom which poetry would inspire and celebrate. But the Revolution turned into the Terror and then into Bona-partism; and it was soon apparent in England that science and industry were together shaping a new world very different from that of the early Romantic dreams. In this world the poet could not be altogether at home; he could not hope to be one of its 'unacknowledged legislators'. But the high Romantic claims for poetry were not readily abandoned; if poetry could not be the inspirer of a brave new world, it could still perhaps offer inspiring comfort in face of the world that was actually growing up.

The highest, most explicit claim of this kind was made by Matthew Arnold; made from a position half in and half out of the Romantic country, from a borderland now deeply shadowed by the advance of science and scepticism. Arnold was himself a divided man: his mother Cornish, his father the formidable Dr. Arnold of Rugby. Standing on Dover beach and looking across the Channel, he speaks with the voice of the onlooker-age:

> The sea of faith
> Was once, too, at the full, and round earth's shore

Lay like the folds of a bright girdle furled.
But now I only hear
Its melancholy, long, withdrawing roar,
Retreating, to the breath
Of the night-wind, down the vast edges drear
And naked shingles of the world.

But Arnold was not, apparently, anxious about the outlook for poetry. "The future of poetry is immense, because in poetry, where it is worthy of its high destinies, our race, as time goes on, will find an ever surer and surer stay. There is not a creed which is not shaken, not an accredited dogma which is not shown to be questionable, not a received tradition which does not threaten to dissolve. . . . More and more mankind will discover that we have to turn to poetry to interpret life for us, to console us, to sustain us."[1]

The view that poetry should be in some sense a moral educator, that it should edify and instruct, was of course familiar long before the Romantic movement; but the claim that it could replace religion in this exacting role was a new Romantic idea, perhaps first advanced by an English poet in Shelley's *Defence of Poetry*. Shelley was sure that his hopes for poetry were in tune with the new age of freedom and progress. Arnold, some fifty years later, could look for no help from the trend of the times. One feels that in making these exacting demands on poetry—in asking it to become a 'complete *magister vitae*', as he once put it—he was speaking with one side of his nature and trying vainly to convince the other half. For he was only in part a moralist and an educator; he was also a Romantic who clung to Romanticism even though he could no longer quite believe in it. And the trouble was that the poetry he ranked most highly for its morally educative power was not the poetry that touched the quick of his response. So in one breath he could affirm that "our only first-rate body of contemporary poetry is the German", and that Goethe is "our greatest modern poet", and in the next breath declare that "Goethe wrote in a style of

[1] From 'The Study of Poetry': *Essays in Criticism*, second series

prose as much as poetry", and that Wordsworth was the greater poet after all.[1]

Goethe and Wordsworth (the young Wordsworth) were for Arnold the two poles of a dilemma that he was perhaps never quite conscious of. Poetry, he feels, has a magical power, but how can this sustain a man in an age of science, which does not recognise anything magical as having any bearing on the bleak unfriendly world, where in the twilight of religious faith life still has to be lived? Or, if poetry is to serve as a moral educator, is it certain that prose—or poetry 'in a style of prose'—will not do as well?

Arnold's dilemma illustrates a weakness in most of these endeavours to defend the claims of poetry against Utilitarian attacks. Except for Coleridge, the defenders never came to grips with the difference between poetry and prose as verbal instruments; and even Coleridge did not go very far into the respective effects of poetry and prose on the reader's mind. Wordsworth agreed with the view expressed in Shelley's *Defence of Poetry*, that "the distinction between poets and prose writers is a vulgar error". Shelley's friend Peacock, against whom he was supposed to be defending poetry, could naturally have asked—why then torture language into the artificial forms of verse?

Valéry's phrase—"A poem is really a kind of machine for producing the poetic state by means of words"—would have grated on Romantic sensibilities, and 'machine' is too crude a term for the actively organised verbal tensions of a poem. But the phrase does indicate that in poetry language has a distinctive function: it is doing something that ordinary prose cannot do and does not generally attempt.

This view had been emphasised and elaborated by the Symbolists, the friends of Valéry's youth; and with them the controversy between the Romantics and the Utilitarians was

[1] See D. G. James, *Matthew Arnold and the Decline of English Romanticism* (Oxford University Press, 1961); Vincent Buckley, *Poetry and Morality* Chatto and Windus, 1959)

revived under new colours, after it had largely died out in England. But in England it came to life again after the first world war, in the form given it by the delayed impact of Symbolism, on the one hand, and by the 'new criticism', influenced by science, on the other. "The past fifty years", Mr. John Press remarks, "have witnessed the attempts of our most gifted poets to incorporate the heritage of Symbolism into the structure of their verse, to express the concepts of a European aesthetic in the native accents of English poetic language."[1]

I want now to look briefly at this 'heritage of Symbolism', in relation particularly to the evolution of consciousness and to the aesthetic controversies of the present day.

[1] *The Fire and the Fountain* (Oxford University Press, 1955), p. 96

VI

After Baudelaire

THE French Symbolist movement, launched with a manifesto by Jean Moréas in 1886, was a resistance movement, easier to describe in terms of its enemies than in terms of its own medley of beliefs. One of its chief enemies was positivism (supposedly scientific), exemplified particularly in the influential writings of Hippolyte Taine. Not only in his *Philosophie de l'Art* (1865), but in his theory that works of art are the strictly determined products of social-economic conditions, and in his treatment of the arts as an inferior kind of science, due to be superseded by it before long, Taine was cut out to infuriate the Symbolists. Equally uncongenial were the complacent bourgeois prosperity of the period, and the French academic attitude towards poetry. These influences created for the Symbolists a stifling atmosphere in which the arts were never valued for themselves but only as servitors of something else—as purveyors of decoration and entertainment, or as educators, though of a rather dubious and inferior kind.

Poetry, in theory, was highly respected; it was part of *la littérature française*. But in practice it was generally treated by critics and professors as a literary exercise which had to observe certain rules and could then be analysed into its component parts and thoughts. The French Romantics had enlarged the bounds of poetic language, but they mostly held to the view that a poet started with certain ideas which he proceeded to clothe in verse. Thus Alfred de Vigny wrote: "I always start from the Idea. Around this centre I evolve a fable which is the demonstration of the thought."

Against all these established attitudes the Symbolists rebelled. They challenged bourgeois society by asserting the right of the artist to live freely by his own values; this led to the conception of the artist as by nature a defiant bohemian, a *poète maudit*, cast out from respectable society and proud of it. They challenged positivism by claiming that the arts gave access to forms of knowledge independent of science and superior to it. They challenged the academic line on poetry by insisting that the function of poetic language, and particularly of images, was not to illustrate ideas but to embody an otherwise indefinable experience.

Valéry said later (adapting a remark by Mallarmé) that "Symbolism can be very simply described as the common intention of several groups of poets (otherwise mutually inimical) to reclaim from music their rightful heritage (*reprendre à la musique leur bien*)".[1] But the Symbolists were not aiming at superficial 'verbal music'; they wanted to imbue their poetry with music's evocatory power.

Wagner's music had great influence on them; so had Schopenhauer and some other German philosophers. Their doctrines were confused; they were always writing articles against each other and splitting into factions. Yet they all looked back to a father-figure, Baudelaire; and through him to much older traditions. These have played a curious role in the history of modern poetry; though with Yeats their direct influence perhaps came, for a time at least, to an end.

Baudelaire had taken from Poe the idea that poetry is a magical instrument for working on the reader's mind (*sorcellerie évocatoire*), and it was easy for him to relate this to various esoteric ideas that were current in the literary Paris of his time. Among his friends and acquaintances were Gérard de Nerval,[2]

---

[1] *A.P.*, p. 42

[2] Gérard de Nerval is now known in this country chiefly for his legendary eccentricities and through a single line of verse made familiar by T. S. Eliot:

Le Prince d'Aquitaine a la tour abolie

But, "though he was not a poet of the first order, he was an innovator who had a decisive influence on modern poetry. The introduction of dreams, myths and the fantasies of the unconscious, which was possible only through the exploration of new resources of language, opened up a vast new seam steeped from early youth in occult writings; Balzac, who drew on Swedenborg for the three novels of his *Livre Mystique;* and the Abbé Constant, who under the name of Eliphas Levi wrote profusely on magic and kindred subjects. All sorts of strange speculations were familiar in this milieu, derived partly from Swedenborg and partly from various esoteric movements which had arisen widely on the Continent during the later 18th century, associated with figures such as Saint-Martin, Pasqualis and Adam Weishaupt.

These movements were a protest against the rationalistic trend of the times, but of course they were not then new-born. They belong to the heretical stream which has always accompanied orthodox religion, sometimes running underground and then re-emerging when conditions were more favourable, or when persons associated with one or other of its currents figured in some way on the public scene. Some of its currents stem from esoteric Christianity and Gnosticism; others from Neoplatonic mysticism or from the ancient religions teachings of the East. Common to most of them was the belief that higher realms of being can be experienced by the aspirant who can raise his consciousness to the required level. They are thus sometimes grouped under the name of Illuminism, a name which dates back to at least the 15th century in Europe.

The 18th century revivals of this tradition were checked by the French Revolution but reappeared soon afterwards, and were passed on to wider circles in France by such writers as Madame de Staël and Joseph de Maistre (of whom Baudelaire spoke, strangely, as "le grand génie de notre temps—un voyant"). Plenty of charlatanry was mixed up with these revivals, and in some of them underground politics played a considerable part. Yet they looked back, I would say, to a genuine ancient wisdom which had sprung originally from earlier modes of consciousness.

---

and added a new dimension to poetry." Martin Turnell, *Baudelaire: a Study of his Poetry* (Hamish Hamilton, 1953), p. 32

Of course, the idea that there once was a genuine ancient wisdom, in possession of some truths forgotten by the modern world, is not very acceptable in the scientific climate of today; a widely held view is that most esoteric movements which cling to such ideas are varieties of the bad old superstitions which haunted mankind before the sun of science rose to drive away the ghosts. As a counter-influence to this assumption, however, a new interest in various forms of mysticism, and in their historical connection with ancient Eastern wisdom, has emerged during recent years. For evidence of this one need only look at publishers' lists, starting perhaps with the appearance in 1946 of Aldous Huxley's anthology, *The Perennial Philosophy*, in the Introduction to which he wrote:

> Rudiments of the Perennial Philosophy may be found among the traditionary lore of primitive peoples in every region of the world, and in its fully developed forms it has a place in every one of the higher religions. A version of the Highest Common Factor in all preceding and subsequent theologies was first committed to writing more than twenty-five centuries ago, and since that time the inexhaustible theme has been treated again and again, from the standpoint of every religious tradition and in all the principal languages of Asia and Europe.[1]

Here, before returning to the main subject of this chapter, I must add two comments. Huxley would probably have regarded the esoteric movements around Baudelaire as forms of occultism which may have owed something to ancient wisdom but had deviated from the one true path; and most followers of his school of thought (including the Vedantists) would agree with him. On the other hand, I would say that their tendency to look to the ancient East as the one true original source of spiritual wisdom is one-sided; it does less than justice, as a rule, to Western and Christian esoteric sources; and it inclines rather often to the dubious belief that old Eastern methods of spiritual

[1] *The Perennial Philosophy* (Chatto and Windus, 1946), p. 1

discipline, which go back to a now long-past stage in the evolution of consciousness, are still quite suitable for modern Western people. But all that is another story.

*   *   *

Nobody can say how far Baudelaire believed in the various esoteric doctrines he absorbed. Like Yeats, he probably took from them whatever he needed for his poetry and his life, without ever quite committing himself to them. They appealed to his love of mystery; and the thought of a world of archetypal beauty, accessible if only in glimpses through the poetry of symbols, was a salve to his life-long feeling of having been cast out from the *vert paradis* of his early childhood. These doctrines were welcome also as a confirmatory background for something he did believe in from his own experience—the magical potency of language.

The most familiar of the esoteric ideas he borrowed is of course that of *correspondances,* developed in detail by Swedenborg but in origin much older. The visible world is held to be a symbolic projection of higher realms. Thus Baudelaire wrote: "Poetry is what is most real, what is completely true only in *another world*. This world, a hieroglyphic dictionary." Or again: "I have long maintained that the poet is *supremely* intelligent; that he is intelligence *par excellence*—and that the imagination is the most *scientific* of faculties, because it alone understands the *universal analogy*, or what mystical religion calls *the correspondence*."

In his own poetry Baudelaire made use mainly of another form of correspondence, between sounds, colours, odours:

> *Les parfums, les couleurs et les sons se répondent*

This synaesthesia is experienced under certain drugs, and Baudelaire's interest in it may have been stimulated by his brief experiments with hashish. It was a subject intensively discussed among the later Symbolists, but it was never very fruitful for their poetry.

Nowadays Baudelaire would no doubt have experimented with mescalin and lysergic acid. The various published accounts of the effects of these drugs (e.g. Aldous Huxley's *The Doors of Perception* and R. H. Ward's *A Drug-Taker's Notes*) show that they produce a remarkable variety of phantasmagoric visions, enchanting, grotesque, or horrible, and sometimes (as with Huxley) brilliantly heightened perceptions of forms and colours in the outer world. This latter effect shows how dependent our normal experience of the outer world is on a particular level of consciousness; it may even suggest that normal consciousness keeps out more than it lets in. But there is no evidence, as far as I know, that these drugs have ever stimulated the writing of good modern poetry.

* * *

Baudelaire was a transcendentalist in his aesthetics, needing no drugs for that; but at the same time his poetry was highly personal; whatever he writes about is infused with his own feelings, ranging between the poles of *extase* and *spleen*. In him there was no conflict between the transcendental and the expression theories; he could speak of poetry being "true only in another world", and yet he could equally well write: "What is the modern conception of pure art? It is to create a suggestive magic containing at one and the same time object and subject, the world which is external to the artist and the artist himself."

If therefore one were asked what Baudelaire's poetry is 'about', one might perhaps say in general terms: about the world, about the poet and about 'another world'. This last phrase is obviously hazardous, inviting misinterpretation, for this other world cannot be defined or described and is not separate from the ordinary world. One can say only that it is what the poet apprehends intuitively when he comes to write, and what a responsive reader will apprehend when he reads. We may call it 'another world' because it is not evident in the external world as generally perceived.

Baudelaire believed in 'another world' sufficiently for his

needs; this may have some bearing on the contrast between his almost classical achievement as poet and critic and the feverish disorder of his short life. His relation to religion was deeply ambivalent, but it probably helped to sustain his belief that poetry has a revelatory power and does not merely induce the poetic state as a private pleasure for individuals.

With Rimbaud and Mallarmé, his two outstanding Symbolist successors, it was different. A note of desperation, apparent in Baudelaire's life but mastered in his poetry, spreads to their work.

Rimbaud wrote: "Baudelaire is the first *voyant*, the king of poets, a true god. But he lived in a too narrowly artistic atmosphere, and the form of his poetry, so highly praised, is paltry (*mesquine*). The invention of the unknown calls for new forms."

Nobody can know exactly what Rimbaud meant by *voyant* here, or in his famous declaration: "Je dis qu'il faut être *voyant*, se faire *voyant*." What would the *voyant* poet see? "Il arrive à l'inconnu, et quand, affolé, il finirait par perdre l'intelligence de ses visions, il les a vues!"

Obviously, Rimbaud felt himself imprisoned by the stuffy bourgeois conventions of his village home, ruled over by his formidably puritanical mother, but there was much more to it than that. Perhaps he was like someone who looks out at the landscape of the world through a dirty, smeared window-pane. He is convinced that if he could clear the pane, the world would spring up in new colours and reveal unknown riches. But the pane is his own consciousness: how can he clear that? He knows that it can be cleared; that at times it has been cleared, when he reads poetry or encounters some other potent stimulus, but not for long. How can he clear it permanently, or at will?

The only method he could think of was through "un long, immense et raisonné dérèglement de tous les sens". The *voyant* state was to be attained, apparently, by disorganising ordinary sense-perceptions, so that a new vision of the world might appear. But what Rimbaud achieved by this means was perhaps not so much a new vision of the world as a series of visions conjured up from his own mind and wide reading and superimposed on the world. Why he turned finally from poetry in his early twenties will never be fully known; perhaps it was partly that he had asked too much of it, and came to realise that after his visions he was still the same man and the world no less a prison. He had never got on with the poets of Paris; he may have come to feel that his own literary pretensions were equally a sham; the only thing was to bury himself in a life of action and hardship where poetry was unknown.

In certain respects Rimbaud reminds me of both Lawrences—D. H. and T. E. Like D. H. Lawrence, he craved for a consciousness not devitalised and sullied over by modern intellectualism, but whereas Lawrence had something of the older participating consciousness as a natural gift, Rimbaud had to fight and exploit himself and others for it, never with a success that satisfied him or did justice to his extraordinary and precocious gifts. Like T. E. Lawrence, he tried to release and accentuate his powers by subjecting his body to harsh experiences, and finally he sought in Ethiopia the anonymity that T. E. Lawrence found in the R.A.F. And, like this Lawrence again, he created and left a legend that exceeded his achievements.

✶   ✶   ✶

In Mallarmé there is equally a note of desperation, but of course in a very different key: the quiet desperation of a respectable schoolmaster who never ceased to dedicate himself to poetry but did cease to believe seriously, it seems, that he would ever complete the legendary *Oeuvre* in which his struggles to liberate poetry from every non-poetic accretion were to culminate. For mingled with his devotion to poetry there was a profound scepticism. He responded to religious ritual, but in much the same way as to Wagnerian music-drama; he spoke of God as "ce vieux et méchant plumage terrassé, heureusement",[1] and

[1] From a letter to Cazalis, 1867, included in *Propos de Poésie,* ed. H. Mondor (Editions du Rocher, Monaco, 1953), p. 87

regarded as illusion any thought of life beyond the grave. He
loathed his work as a schoolmaster and cared for little in contemporary life outside the circle of devoted friends who
gathered on Tuesday evenings to hear his gnomic monologues
(of which no record, alas, remains) at his flat in the rue de
Rome. Since he saw no hope for man in this world or any other,
the only thing was to create a world, a world of ideal beauty
that could be experienced through poetry: but even this could
be no more than a consoling dream. The reality was nothingness (*le Rien* or *le Néant*), and even the purest poems could be
no more than a 'glorious lie'.[1]

De l'éternel azur la sereine ironie. . . .

*　　*　　*

In these three poets, Baudelaire, Rimbaud, Mallarmé, one can
perhaps see an endeavour to recover not only the musical
rights of poetry (as Valéry put it), but the rights of poetry itself.
They had in common one belief: a belief in the magical
incantatory power of poetry to induce a vision of some ideal
realm. In earlier times this view of poetry did not have to be
advanced as a rather novel theory, nor was it necessary for
poetry to reclaim its own from music. The earliest languages of
which we have any glimpse were themselves song-like, and to
suppose that poetry has developed out of prosaic speech is to
look at it the wrong way round. Prosaic speech has developed
out of poetry, leaving poetry on an eminence which gradually
became more lonely and farther removed from the plains of
discourse.

During the 18th century, with the rise of the onlooker-
consciousness, the tendency was to regard the eminence as
dubious territory and to cultivate elegant forms of verse which
mostly kept to the plains. The Romantics set out to reconquer
the eminence, but they could not always see their way through
the clouds. The Symbolists set their habitation there and sought

[1] *Ibid.*, p. 66

to recover, as a conscious technique, the ancient magic of the place; but the air was thin and the abyss threatening; few could dwell on that height for long without some loss of nerve. "We only traverse the idea of perfection as a hand passes with impunity through a flame; but the flame is uninhabitable, and dwelling places on the serene heights are of necessity deserted."[1]

Baudelaire had some belief in the objective existence of the ideal realm; if Rimbaud ever held such a belief, he soon lost it; Mallarmé never had it. During those years, covering the last two-thirds of the 19th century, the climate of consciousness was becoming progressively unfavourable, and to justify poetry as more than a recreation was becoming increasingly hard.

I am not suggesting that if Rimbaud and Mallarmé had held religious beliefs, they could have written more or better poetry: this is an entirely individual question, unpredictable either way. But their relations to poetry might have been less tormented; they would not have treated poetry as the one remaining hope in an alien world. If poetry is made a substitute for religion, it is likely either to degenerate into moralistic discourse, or to break under the strain.

Mallarmé talked and wrote extensively on the theory of poetry, but it might be a mistake to suppose that he evolved his theories largely out of his head. His approach to language was not so much that of an intellectual theorist as that of an almost mystical explorer; he sought to gain awareness of the subtle activities and interplay of words within his own mind. In some of his essays and letters he tried to describe the curious experiences he encountered; we will come to these later on.

*   *   *

Valéry has described his last visit to Mallarmé, on a burning July day in 1898.[2] Spread out on the table in the tiny study of Mallarmé's country cottage were the sheets of *Un Coup de Dés*, where the inner form and movement of the poem were to be

[1] Valéry; *A.P.*, p. 46
[2] *Dernière Visite à Mallarmé.* (Variété II)

rendered in the specially designed typography of the printed page. Valéry at that time was writing nothing; there seemed to him a kind of contrast between the practice of literature and the pursuit of perfect rigour and sincerity in thinking. He had wished to lay these doubts before Mallarmé—"je l'aimais et je le plaçais au-dessus de tous"—but it was a delicate question and he had always hesitated, waiting for a better moment.

In the evening, still brilliant and warm, Valéry was accompanied by Mallarmé to the railway-station. The harvest fields were touched with gold and Mallarmé remarked on it—"le premier coup de cymbale de l'automne sur la terre". But when autumn came, he had gone.

VII

Science and Semantics

AFTER Mallarmé's death it seemed that the Symbolist movement was over, as though passing with him into the *silence* and *absence* he had cherished. In France this was largely true, but Symbolist influence was soon to cross the Channel and (after an incubation period prolonged by the 1914-18 war) to bear fruit in the 'new poetry' inaugurated chiefly by T. S. Eliot and Ezra Pound. Arthur Symons's book, *The Symbolist Movement in Literature*, came out in 1902, with a second edition in 1908. Eliot has written of it: "I owe Mr. Symons a great debt. But for having read his book I should not, in the year 1908, have heard of Laforgue and Rimbaud; and but for reading Verlaine I should not have heard of Corbière. So this Symons book is one of those which have affected the course of my life."[1]

This new poetry of images and broken syntax was by no means so unintelligible as its first angry critics claimed, but after the Georgian verse which had up to then represented 'modern poetry' it was hard going, and the credo that accompanied it was certainly confusing. This is a well-known story; I want only to mention a few relevant points.

The new movement (influenced in this respect by T. E. Hulme) declared itself to be anti-Romantic. It attacked worn-out verbiage and the cult of personal feeling. But the new poetry was obviously not 'classical' in any accepted sense. It showed no respect for the classical canons of formal order and logical sense. The Eliot of those days could be regarded as a classicist in his criticism and a modern Romantic in his poetry. *The Waste Land* was intellectual in its recondite allusions; anti-intellectual in its remoteness from prose discourse.

The event that set the key for most of the ensuing critical

[1] *See* J. Isaacs, *The Background of Modern Poetry* (Bell, 1951)

debates was the encounter of the new poetry with the new criticism, often dated from the appearance in 1924 (two years after *The Waste Land*) of I. A. Richards's *Principles of Literary Criticism*. In origins and outlook the new criticism had very little in common with the new poetry; its first aim was to get away from gossipy personal impressions and to give critical method a sound basis in science and semantics. Thus one might have expected it to prefer the rational to the magical element in poetry and not to look kindly on poems showing Symbolist influence. In fact, the new critics were mostly on the side of the new poetry, at first. They welcomed its reinvigoration of poetic language, compared with the genteel diction of the lesser Georgians; and the denunciation of it by the literary Establishment seemed to guarantee its credentials as a voice of the new post-war world.

Yet there was a conflict latent here, the conflict that Valéry encountered in himself; that drove him to make contradictory remarks about poetry and to doubt whether there was much future for it in a scientific age. It was a conflict first plainly heard when the Utilitarians decried Romantic poetry; it became a strong issue among the Symbolists; and it was bound to emerge again when the new critics got to grips with the new poetry. To a strictly rationalist approach the magical element will seem meaningless, probably irritating. But a scientifically-minded critic who responds to poetry cannot help recognising the potency of the magical element; can he account for it in rational terms?

This is what Richards set out to do. He dismisses all talk of a special 'aesthetic emotion' or 'aesthetic state': these are bogus entities which merely shelve the problem and are of no aid to a scientific treatment of it.[1] He then develops a theory, based on

---

[1] All the same, when Richards comes to speak of what poetry actually does, his account is not so very far removed from Valéry's. Thus in the *Principles* (p. 245) he writes of "the heightened power of combining all the effects of formal elements into a single response, which the poet bestows. To point out that the 'sense of musical delight is a gift of the imagination' was one of Coleridge's most brilliant feats."

neurology, whereby a work of art gives pleasure and is valued because it induces a maximum degree of harmony among impulses (or 'appetencies') which normally conflict with and frustrate one another.

One difficulty with this theory is that it hardly seems to be borne out by observation: the persons most open to frequent aesthetic stimuli are not always notable for order and harmony in their lives. Often it seems, on the contrary, that the experience of order and harmony which is given by works of art may make the ordinary untidy world *more* difficult to live in.

But the powerful first impression made by the *Principles* can be understood. Richards had already achieved an arcane reputation with *The Meaning of Meaning*, written in collaboration with C. K. Ogden. And now, at a time when the Romantic claims for poetry seemed to be crumbling, he came forward with new scientific reasons for placing a very high practical value on poetry and all the arts.

His neurological theory has not held its ground, and probably Richards would no longer endorse it himself. But the tone and temper of the *Principles*, its endeavour to apply modern scientific knowledge to aesthetic problems, were an impetus which encouraged the new criticism to draw equipment from a variety of research fields. From Richards, too, especially from his later book, *Practical Criticism*, it gained one of its watchwords, 'close reading'—paying close attention to the text and not relying on a vaguely emotional response.[1]

In this country, the second main influence on criticism between the wars came, of course, from F. R. Leavis and his Cambridge school. Here, too, there was insistence on close disciplined reading, but with a difference in canons of valuation. Leavis has not always written kindly of Matthew Arnold, but as an educator and moralist he is in the Arnold line. For him, the prime virtue of great literature is that it is life-enhancing; it

[1] For a useful survey of some of the chief modern schools of criticism (especially the American), see Stanley Edgar Hyman, *The Armed Vision* (New York, Vintage Books, 1955)

embodies and instils healthy moral attitudes, so that those who respond to its influence are helped to face the tragic human situation with insight and courage.

The same difficulty that confronted Arnold arises here. If great literature has above all a morally educative function, is there a special need for poetry? Will not prose do as well? And perhaps it is significant that in later years Leavis came to find "the central tradition of English literary values . . . exhibited in the novel more forcefully and completely than in formal poetry".[1]

Of course, I am not pretending to dispose of the new criticism with these cursory few words. It has greatly extended the range of critical techniques; close reading can be a salutary corrective to lazy reading; and close criticism can be helpful in making difficult poems more accessible.[2] All this may be agreed, and yet one can add that in pedantic hands these methods may do harm by diverting the reader from what he must finally do for himself: encounter the poem with nothing between him and it. A constant preoccupation with analysis may weaken the capacity for direct experience. Studying the menu becomes so absorbing that one forgets to eat.

Perhaps in this country there has been a certain reluctance to deal directly with anything that sounds so precious, so outmoded and ninety-ish, as the 'poetic state'. Richards did deal with it, but by the debunking method of denying that there was anything unusual about it. After that the trend was towards a more robust concern with close reading on the one hand, and on the other with health-giving moral influences. So in this respect the situation is much where Valéry left it: science cannot make much sense of the 'poetic state', and for an English critic the best thing may be to say very little about it. Even in the writing of poetry the most recent tendency has been to regard the magical element as dubious and to prefer either a modest

---

[1] Vincent Buckley, *Poetry and Morality* (Chatto and Windus, 1959), p. 180

[2] See *Interpretations,* edited by John Wain (Routledge, 1955)

descriptive kind of verse that takes no risks, or a kind of tough informal rhetoric.[1]

Some headway has been made, however, in dealing with what poetry communicates. We have got away from the crude form of the expression theory, according to which a poet's personal feelings are poured out into his verse. Eliot, in a well-known passage, put this reaction in a perhaps deliberately extreme form:

> Poetry is not a turning loose of emotion, but an escape from emotion; it is not the expression of personality, but an escape from personality. . . . The emotion of art is impersonal. And the poet cannot reach this impersonality without surrendering himself wholly to the work to be done.[2]

If this account is meant to present the artist as a purely selfless creator, it can never be entirely true. But it certainly is true that the emotion which enters into the genesis of a poem may have no obvious relation to the poet's personal feelings at the time. Often the poem will come from an unconscious spring, and may finally stand before the poet as an unfamiliar creation which he can hardly recognise as belonging to himself.

Perhaps this is how the expression theory ought to be put—a poem does express a poet's emotion, but an unconscious emotion? That is of course roughly the Freudian view: the artist relieves his unconscious tensions by projecting them into his work. Certainly this happens, and perhaps in some degree it always happens. But the Freudian theory, often penetrating on the genesis of works of art, fails to account for the pleasure

[1] "Over forty years ago two Americans and an Irishman attempted to put English poetry back into the mainstream of European culture. The effect of those generations who have succeeded to the heritage of Eliot, Pound and Yeats has been largely to squander the awareness these three gave us of our place in world literature, and to retreat into a self-congratulatory parochialism." Charles Tomlinson, 'Poetry To-Day', in *The Modern Age* (Pelican Guide to English Literature, volume seven, edited by Boris Ford), 1961

[2] From 'Tradition and the Individual Talent', first published in *The Sacred Wood*, 1920. Reprinted in *Selected Essays* (Faber, 1932)

given by their harmonious formal structure, or for their awakening effect on *perception* (a point to which I shall return). Freud seems to have regarded aesthetic pleasure as something of a 'mystery', but he thought it might be interpreted as a kind of bait (a 'forepleasure') whereby we are enticed into letting a work of art bring about in us the same kind of emotional release which the creation of it provided for the artist. Something like this release may occur, but it is not all that occurs, nor does it seem to me that we read poetry in order to obtain it.[1]

★   ★   ★

For the best examination of the expression theory we must turn to America and Mrs. Susanne Langer.[2] She distinguishes the 'import' of a poem from its discursive meaning; its import is apprehended by intuition, defined simply as an immediate grasping—"the same sort of insight that makes language more than a stream of little squeaks". In reading prose discourse, she says, we apprehend its meaning by building up successive intuitions as we go along, while aesthetic intuition is first and foremost the intuition of a whole, a *Gestalt*; the import resides in the whole and will vanish if we try to analyse the whole into components. Thus the import of a poem is lost in a prose paraphrase.

Mrs. Langer speaks also of "vital import", because "it is always some mode of feeling, sense, emotion, consciousness,

[1] "What is most important about this thing we call a work of art, that is admittedly a symbol, is not the original primary unconscious wish or wishes that it symbolises, but the fact that a new thing has been created. A new bit of the outside world, which is not the original primary object of the wish, has been made interesting and significant." Marion Milner, 'Psycho-Analysis and Art', from *Psycho-Analysis and Contemporary Thought*, ed. John D. Sutherland (Hogarth Press and Institute of Psycho-Analysis, 1958), p. 99

[2] Her three relevant (and highly stimulating) books, first published in the United States, came out in this country as follows: *Philosophy in a New Key* (Oxford University Press, 1951); *Feeling and Form* (Routledge, 1953); *Problems of Art* (Routledge, 1957)

that is conveyed by a successful work of art". Not, however, the artist's "own actual feelings, but what he knows about feeling. Once in possession of a rich symbolism, that knowledge may actually exceed his entire personal experience. . . . As soon as the natural forms of subjective experience are abstracted to the point of symbolic presentation, we can use these forms to *imagine* feeling and understand its nature. Self-knowledge, insight into all phases of life and mind, spring from artistic imagination. That is the cognitive value of the arts."[1]

This version of the expression theory (derived from Mrs. Langer's earlier studies in the Cassirer school of symbolic forms) is obviously a great improvement on the Romantic theory of poetry as individual self-expression. It clarifies the difference (or at least one difference) between the language of poetry and the language of prose; it brings out the kind of thing a work of art is—not an imitation or description of anything, but a symbolic formal structure, a created *Gestalt*; and it shows that poetry does not merely give a peculiar private pleasure but leads to a certain enlargement of knowledge—knowledge of "the dynamics of subjective experience, the pattern of vitality, sentience, feeling and emotion".

All this seems to me true, as far as it goes, but I think it fails to cover some essential points. Mrs. Langer presents the reader of a poem as achieving his act of intuitive grasping by his own efforts entirely; she pays very little attention to the action of the poem on his consciousness. Yet it is there, in the mind, that the poem is experienced, and there that it actively creates the possibility of experiencing it. Also, what we gain an intuition of through a poem is not *only* a pattern of sentience; a poem can also give us new or heightened perceptions of the outer world. Mrs. Langer does not altogether deny this, but she brings it within the compass of the expression theory by accepting the commonly held view that images from the outer world are then being used simply as symbols of the poet's feelings—the "subjectivisation of nature", she calls it.

[1] All my quotations are from *Problems of Art*

I will return to these points from a different angle; but first, to gather up a few threads.

★   ★   ★

The life and writings of Valéry typify an unresolved conflict between a scientific way of thinking and the symbolic power of poetry. It is a conflict that was bound to arise in our epoch: the epoch of the onlooker-consciousness. In earlier periods poetry had been accepted quite naturally as a form of utterance that bore witness to the higher realms from which it was inspired. With the onset of the onlooker-consciousness, this belief lost ground; experience no longer seemed to support it. It was revived, in an ambivalent way, by Baudelaire, and it continued to influence the Symbolists, but with them it was intellectualised into aesthetic theories, leading to the final obscurity of Mallarmé, and later to Valéry's opinion that poetry had no significance beyond the peculiar pleasure it gave to its devotees.

Meanwhile, during the 19th century in England, the outlook for poetry had come into question; Arnold tried to justify poetry on morally educative grounds. With the decline of Romanticism, these questionings lapsed; but they arose again when, in our own century, Symbolist influence led to a new English poetry based on images and evocation. The new criticism tried to bring scientific methods to bear on the new poetry, while the Arnoldian way of looking to literature for moral education was revived, together with a new discipline of reading, by Leavis and his associates.

All along there have been two broad schools of criticism (not rigidly separate), one emphasising the rational meaning of poetry, the other its magical-symbolic meaning. Few critics have gone so far as to claim that one or other meaning has *no* value, though even this has been done.[1] "A good deal of the

---

[1] In 1760 d'Alembert wrote: "Here, in my opinion, is the strict but just rule that our century imposes on poets: it now recognises as good in verse only what it would find excellent in prose." The present-day American critic, Yvor Winters, is a firm exponent of rather similar views. A. E.

best modern criticism", Professor Frank Kermode remarks, "is interesting as evidence of the oscillations and tensions in the minds of critics between the claims of the Image and the claims of ordinary discourse. These tensions are visible also in poetry, and it is possible that in the controlling of them the immediate future of poetry lies, as well as our criticism and ways of looking at the past."[1]

For the first school, the problem is to show why as a moral educator poetry can do better than prose. For the second, the problem is to show why the magical meaning is important, except as a source of private aesthetic pleasure.

It may be useful now to approach these unanswered questions from the reader's side, and to consider in an elementary way how words are handled in the mind when any reading (whether of poetry or of prose) is going on.

Housman, on the other hand, argued in a celebrated lecture that lines which make no rational sense can still be 'ravishing poetry'.

[1] *Romantic Image* (Routledge, 1957), p. 153

PART II
WORDS FROM BEHIND

VIII

The Quick Brown Fox

ANY attempt to describe how words behave when poetry is read has to depend on that treacherous process, introspection; but anyone able to see and hear words with the mind's eye and ear will probably have rather similar encounters with them.

To hear words clearly in the mind is the first requirement for ease in handling them. (This resembles, but may be quite distinct from, the capacity to hear music inwardly, which is what a 'good ear for music' primarily means: some poets—e.g. Yeats—have had a poor ear for music.) The words must also linger long enough in the mind for the sound of a word near the end of a sentence, say, to be compared with the sound of a word at the beginning. But words are not taken into the mind exactly *as* words, spoken or written, but as a combination of sound and image, and with something added—a kind of inner life or active quality that belongs to almost every word and becomes apparent (modified by its context if it has one) when the word is inwardly experienced. And this active quality gives to the inwardly perceived word a certain mobile shape.

To be able mentally to visualise words is useful for spelling, but for handling them one needs also some perception of their actively mobile shapes and qualities, for it is these which have to be related and compared when it is a question of finding or choosing words for special purposes, or of judging the inner harmonies of words when they are read.

Let us take a familiar sentence—

The quick brown fox jumps over the lazy dog

—and examine each word in turn. This will be laborious, but if we are to approach the use of words in poetry it seems best to start on the ground floor.

75

We can omit 'the' as a word with no strong character of its own, serving here to generalise the sentence. But worth noting is the difference between starting the sentence with 'The' and starting it with 'A'. If we write "A quick brown fox . . .", the 'A' turns it into an individual instance and the whole sentence starts up in brighter colours.

quick—A sharp word with a pointed, darting shape.

brown—In *this* context, tawny, because of the link with 'fox'. By itself it is darker, duller; shapeless because spread over a surface.

fox—It can of course call up a picture of a fox, but that is to get away from the character of the word itself. Another sharp-pointed word; bristly, quivering, like a nose exploring the air.

jumps—Looks like an inverted u, tilted forward ⋂ and held in tension, ready for release.

over—Neutral in colour, arched in shape. In some other contexts it would have a wider sweep, curving away into the distance. In looking at it here one has to keep it free from the associations of other meanings. In "all is over between us", it acquires from its different context a drooping shape. In the cricket 'over', a semi-technical usage, the word has for me no discernible shape or character of its own; it simply calls up the picture of a cricket-field.

We can pass over the second 'the' and come on to *lazy*. A pungent word, with a languorous, gradually uncoiling shape.

dog—Here the word has a blunt, stubby shape. Again necessary to keep it free from irrelevant associations and dog-images.

Perhaps these impressions are simply personal associations, foisted on to the words? Very likely some or all of the words would look rather different to someone else. But the impressions are not inventions. The shapes are what I see in the mind's eye when I silently repeat the words, while at the same time hearing them in the mind's ear.

Of course, if one reads the sentence through in the normal way, the shapes and gestures of the individual words pass by too quickly to be seized. But I think they play into the act of

76

apprehension, and contribute to the total effect of the sentence. The point I am suggesting is that in any such act of apprehension one is not dealing with words in the ordinary literal sense, but with the shapes and characters they disclose when taken into the mind and inwardly observed.

The total effect of the sentence on me is mildly agreeable. It has a variety of vowel sounds, and it opens appropriately with a rapid movement which slows down and gathers weight with the last few syllables. There is, too, a touch of fantasy about it which draws it away from strictly factual prose and carries it towards the borders of poetry. It could indeed be read as a metrical line, and if the word order were changed—

> Over the lazy dog the quick brown fox
> Jumps.

—it would pass as a fragment from a modest piece of blank verse. In this case, 'jumps' comes into the mind with an effective thud. The word keeps its springy shape, but curving quickly from it is a trajectory that falls to earth.

★   ★   ★

Before coming to the reading of poetry, we ought to consider the writing of it. Nowadays there is a view that anyone who writes poetry is doing something quite ordinary, not very different from talking or writing a letter; but the testimony of poets hardly seems to bear this out.

The first element in the writing of a poem may be a rhythm without words. Eliot says:

> I know that a poem, or a passage of a poem, may tend to realise itself first as a particular rhythm before it reaches expression in words, and that this rhythm may bring to birth the idea and the image; and I do not believe that this is an experience peculiar to myself.[1]

[1] 'The Music of Poetry' (1942). Reprinted in *On Poetry and Poets* (Faber, 1957), p. 38

Valéry speaks of a similar experience:

> My poem *Le Cimetière Marin* began in me with a rhythm, that of a French line . . . of ten syllables, divided into four and six. I had as yet no idea with which to fill out the form. Gradually a few hovering words settled in, little by little determining the subject, and my labour (a very long labour) was before me.[1]

These passages are familiar, but the process they describe is strange. One might suppose that the unconscious has something to say and is calling attention to it by insinuating this rhythm, like a drum-beat, into the conscious mind. But the rhythm is more than a signal; it belongs in some way to the words which are going to be found. Perhaps some of the words are already present in the unconscious, and it is only their rhythm that can at first get through; they emerge when the poet gives his mind to the rhythm, lets it penetrate him and invites it, as it were, to speak.

Probably the inception of a poem through a rhythm alone is relatively rare. More often a poem starts with a line or phrase (Valéry's *ligne donnée*) which comes into the mind from 'nowhere', or it may be a visual image or a vaguely apprehended idea, probably accompanied in most cases by a faint stir of emotion:

> As I went along, thinking of nothing in particular, only looking at things around me and following the progress of the seasons, there would flow into my mind, with sudden and unaccountable emotion, sometimes a line or two of verse, sometimes a whole stanza at once, accompanied, not preceded, by a vague notion of the poem which they were destined to form part of. . . . So far as I can make out, the source of the suggestions thus proffered to the brain was an abyss I have already had occasion to mention, the pit of the stomach.[2]

[1] *A.P.*, p. 80

[2] A. E. Housman, *The Name and Nature of Poetry* (Cambridge University Press, 1934)

Occasionally the poem may be written quickly, in a state bordering on trance.[1] More commonly the given phrase serves only as an initiating impulse. It may suggest what the poem is going to be about; then the poet has to induce the suggestion to grow and flower and take form in his mind. This is not simply an exercise in craftsmanship (though craftsmanship, sometimes laborious, will probably be needed later), but of discovering what the given line signifies; of compelling it to summon further words or lines.

This process resembles (though it generally has more pressure behind it) the everyday effort to find a word for something you want to say, or to recall a name. You hold on to some clue or association, or perhaps a mental picture, and suddenly, if you are lucky, the word or name emerges, like a bubble appearing from 'nowhere' in a glass of soda-water. But in this case the word or name is familiar, an old friend. A phrase that is searched for by a poet may, when it finally breaks surface, give symbolic expression to something he has never laid hold of before. "The process of writing a poem—in many instances—consists of cajoling an unembodied something into its incarnation. . . . Before it has found itself in words by finding the words for itself, that *something else* has as little character, is as indescribable, as a name that we are failing to recall."[2]

The effort of search can sometimes be felt as a tension between two points or poles inside the head—not as a physical sensation, exactly, but with a location somewhere behind the forehead. Each pole is associated with something that may itself be a word,

[1] For some modern instances of poems written in this way, see Robin Skelton, *The Poetic Pattern* (Routledge, 1956). Herbert Read has said: "I can aver that all the poetry I have written which I continue to regard as authentic poetry was written immediately, instantaneously, in a condition of trance." (*Collected Essays in Literary Criticism*; Faber, 1938; p. 110.) Cf. also Stephen Spender, *The Making of a Poem* (Hamish Hamilton, 1955); Rosamund Harding, *The Anatomy of Inspiration* (Heffer, revised edition, 1948); Brewster Ghiselin (ed.), *The Creative Process: a Symposium* (Mentor Books, New York, 1955)

[2] I. A. Richards, *The Screens* (Routledge, 1960), p. 122

or an image, or a vaguely apprehended thought. The effort consists in concentrating on the *relation* between the two words or images or thoughts, a relation that has to do with their significance in connection with each other, and out of the tension of this relation the required word or phrase, somehow expressing this significance, has to be born:

> . . . and gives to airy nothing
> A local habitation, and a name.

Thus the finding of the right word is not only a process of mentally running over a number of possible words and choosing the best, though this may often have to be done. A word or phrase is found also by concentrating on what has to be expressed and persuading the word to crystallise out of that. Sometimes words which may seem strange or even inappropriate individually will be recognised as the right words because of their inward relationships.

Years ago I read in a book of war memoirs (I can't recall the title or author): "The men's voices came oddly out of the fog, like jokes out of eternity." The simile would be difficult to justify on logical grounds, yet it struck me as having a kind of rightness, as though there were an inner relationship between the two sets of words. And it would hardly have occurred to the author unless 'voices—oddly—out of the fog' had set up in his mind a relationship which brought forth 'jokes—eternity' as somehow corresponding to it.

*   *   *

Now the reader takes the poem into his mind. He may grasp the rational meaning at once, or some or even all of it may at first elude him.[1] But in any event the active principles of the words (their individual meanings, together with their shapes

---

[1] In *The Use of Poetry* (1933), Eliot wrote: "I know that some of the poetry to which I am most devoted is poetry which I did not understand at first reading; some is poetry which I am not sure I understand yet: for instance, Shakespeare's."

and sounds) will be forming a pattern in his mind. It is the pattern formed originally in the poet's mind as a result of his efforts to lay hold of whatever vague impulse or apprehension or image may have prompted him to write. Thus when the pattern is reproduced in the reader's mind, he can immediately encounter, *through* it, something of the poet's original experience. It is in this way, perhaps, that a poem can communicate a preliminary experience before it is rationally understood.

But this will not happen unless a change in the reader's consciousness is brought about. The poet writes from a state of mind which is open to non-verbal apprehensions. Once he has compelled whatever he apprehends to take form in a pattern, a tension, of verbal relationships, he has created an instrument which can act on the reader's mind and open it to the same kind of inner perception. In reading poetry there is this feeling, almost physical, of opening; the tension of verbal relationships is the door.

Through this door one enters a region that lies behind words. One realises that the word on the page is an inert copy of the real word which comes to life in the mind, actively expressing its meaning and shooting out its feelers, its links of association, which relate it in dynamic interplay with other words.[1]

[1] "It is no empty figure of speech to assert that the language of poems can make us see an interplay of relationships or that relationships seen by the mind are not immovable, like the bricks of an edifice. Relationships are not so much like bricks, as like a Maenad's hair floating in the wind, and in a poem many winds blow at once." Winifred Nowotny, *The Language Poets Use.* (University of London: Athlone Press, 1962), p. 97

IX

Chance and Artifice

IT is this region behind words that Mallarmé was drawn to explore; he may have pressed farther into it than anyone else has consciously done. "Mallarmé," Valéry says, "had made for himself a sort of science of *his* words. There is no doubt that he gave his mind to a study of their forms, explored the interior space where they appear, now as *causes* and now as *effects*; estimated what one might call their *poetic charges*; and that, through this never-ending work of precision, words came to be secretly ordered under the *power* of his spirit, in accordance with a mysterious law of his profound sensibility."[1]

Mallarmé's wish—at least in later life—was not so much to write personal poetry as to become a vehicle for poetry; sometimes he seems to have believed that if he could evoke the primal purity and power of words, the words themselves would almost write a poem:

> L'oeuvre pure implique la disparition élocutoire du poète, qui cède l'initiative aux mots, par le heurt de leur inégalité mobilisés; ils s'allument de reflets réciproques comme une virtuelle traînée de feux sur des pierreries, remplaçant la respiration perceptible en l'ancien souffle lyrique ou la direction personnelle enthousiaste de la phrase.[2]

[1] *Je disais à Stéphane Mallarmé.* (Variété III)

[2] From 'Crise de Vers' in *Divagations* (Paris: Bibliothèque Charpentier; first published in 1897). Mallarmé's prose is almost as resistant to translation as his poetry; a rough rendering of this passage might be: "A pure work implies the disappearance of the poet as speaker, he cedes the initiative to words, mobilised by the shock of their unequal encounters; they catch fire by reflection from each other, like a virtual trail of jewel-flashes, replacing the old breath of lyrical inspiration and the assiduous personal shaping of the phrase."

Probably most writers have experienced something of this kind. It can seem at times that the words are taking charge, choosing themselves, dictating the course of the writing. But if words are given their head, they are liable to get too far away from their ordinary meanings. The result may be brilliantly original; or more probably, when viewed coolly from the outside, it may seem exaggerated or grotesque.

Perhaps a composer may have a similar experience, but if so he will need to be equally on guard with it. Where, however, he does have an advantage, from Mallarmé's point of view, is that musical notes are pure symbols, with no referential meaning, and Mallarmé, an assiduous listener to music, was led or misled to dream of a poetry which would not only approach but actually attain to this condition. His obvious difficulty was that words never can be divorced from their referential meanings—or poetry could be made out of harmonious nonsense-syllables.[1] This difficulty he called *le hasard*: a word needed for its sound or its inner quality may have an ordinary meaning that is not quite right, or a word with the right meaning may have the wrong sound. Thus Mallarmé speaks of the *hasard* which clings to words "in spite of the artifice of dipping them alternately in meaning and sonority". For a long time he may have hoped that *le hasard* could be excluded by devising a new, incantatory form of language; but in the end he was driven to conclude that "Jamais un coup de dés n'abolira le hasard"—by no stroke of fortune can the utilitarian awkwardness of words be overcome.

I think Mallarmé was misguided in treating *le hasard* simply as an obstacle: for the poet it can be an opportunity he would not wish to avoid. His work is to bring the two kinds of meaning, the referential and the symbolic, into kindling conjunction, so that the referential meaning is enriched and the two

[1] Purely incantatory forms of words can exist, in some Eastern mantrams or in magical spells, but the onlooker mode of consciousness is not as susceptible to them as were some earlier modes; and in any event they are distinct from the human language of poetry.

meanings strike sparks from one another. If he treats one or other meaning as unimportant, he will veer towards either the prosaic or the meaningless.

Mallarmé, however, had an extraordinary, a religious, faith in the magical power and virtue of words. He seems to have believed that through their inner relations they could disclose a realm of ideal beauty, and that the only purpose of the universe was to create such a realm through the human agency of poets; or through an archetypal book to which would belong the *grand oeuvre* he always hoped to write. "*Tout, au monde, existe pour aboutir à un livre.*"[1]

A fantastic, almost paranoiac belief, one might feel; but I think Mallarmé did not simply invent it. It arose from his interpretation of the experiences that came to him as an explorer of the region behind words. The experiences began when at the age of about twenty-four he was starting to work on his *Hérodiade*. He was living at Tournon as an unhappy young schoolmaster, unable to keep order and hating his job.[2] In 1866 he wrote to Henri Cazalis:

> I will tell you that for the past month I have been among the purest glaciers of the Aesthetic—that after having found the Void (*le Néant*) I found the beautiful—and you cannot imagine into what lucid altitudes I am venturing.

Nine months later, also to Cazalis:

> I have made a sufficiently long descent into the Void to be able to speak with certainty. There is nothing but Beauty—and it has only one perfect expression: Poetry.

[1] Not a book written only by himself, but a work to which all true poets have tried to contribute without knowing it. Mallarmé spoke also of the 'great work' in the sense of the alchemists, 'our ancestors': as an operation which would effect the transmutation and redemption of language. See A. R. Chisholm, *Mallarmé's Grand Oeuvre* (Manchester University Press, 1962)

[2] "Car je suis peu respecté, et même, parfois, accablé de papier mâché et de huées." (Letter to Henri Cazalis, July 1865)

A year later again, this time to François Coppée:

> And now, having arrived at the horrible vision of a pure work,
> I have almost lost my reason and the meanings of the most
> familiar words.[1]

He adds that after these ordeals he felt so estranged from himself
that he was able to recover a sense of personal identity only by
looking at his face in a mirror—or "I would have become
again the Void".

Later I will try to throw a little light on these disturbing
experiences from quite another angle. With Mallarmé they
arose, I think, from his intense effort to penetrate deeply into the
region behind words and to bring their relation-patterns clearly
before his inner sight. Beyond them, deeper still, there was
nothing, the Void; for Mallarmé believed in nothing else.

In later life he seems never to have carried his explorations so
far as to feel himself threatened by them in this way, but in his
prose essays there are fragmentary passages where he speaks of
the same kind of inner vision. One of the best known of these is:

> A quoi bon la merveille de transposer un fait de nature en sa
> presque disparition vibratoire selon le jeu de la parole,
> cependant; si ce n'est pour qu'en émane, sans la gêne d'un
> proche ou concret rappel, la notion pure.
> Je dis: une fleur! et, hors de l'oubli où ma voix relègue aucun
> contour, en tant que quelque chose d'autre que les calices sus,
> musicalement se lève, l'idée même et suave, l'absente de tous
> bouquets.[2]

[1] Quotations from *Propos sur la Poésie*, collected and edited by Henri
Mondor (Monaco, Editions du Rocher, 1953)

[2] "What good is the marvel of transposing a natural fact into a transient
vibration, vanishing almost in the play of words, unless for the purpose of
causing to emanate from it, without the distraction of a close or concrete
recall, the pure notion.

I say: a flower! and disregarding the oblivion into which my voice
relegates every shape, something other than the known calyx arises musically,
the fragrant idea itself, absent from all bouquets." (From 'Crise de Vers', in
Divagations, op. cit.)

Here Mallarmé seems to be saying that a poem about a flower ought to call up an inner vision not of any particular flower, but of an archetypal, Platonic flower, of which all actual flowers are imperfect representations. In his realm of ideal beauty, only the archetypal flower can exist; and in some realm it may exist. But how impoverished poetry would be if it could not illumine in detail all the extraordinary varieties of flowers on earth!

If Mallarmé means that he was able to call up the archetypal image in himself simply by repeating the words, *une fleur*, this would certainly imply a rare gift. For myself, the inner impression is not of the 'idea' of a flower, but merely of the shape and quality of the word, flower. And incidentally this is different from the inner aspect of *fleur*, which for me has a more graceful shape, as of a flower opening, and a lighter quality; 'flower' is richer and a little heavier, as of a bell-shaped flower curving downwards from a stalk. One of the insuperable problems of translation is that an English word may be in usage the exact equivalent of a foreign word and yet may be experienced differently in the mind.[1]

Another cryptic passage in the same essay has been variously interpreted:

Décadente, Mystiques, les Ecoles se déclarant ou étiquetées en hâte par notre presse d'information, adoptent, comme rencontre, le point d'un Idealisme qui (pareillement aux fugues, aux sonates) refuse les matériaux naturels et, comme brutale, une pensée exacte les ordonnant; pour ne garder rien que la suggestion. Instituer une relation entre les images exacte, et que s'en détache un tiers aspect fusible et clair présenté à la divination. . . . Abolie, la prétension, esthetiquement une erreur, quoiqu'elle régit les chefs-d'oeuvre, d'inclure au papier subtil du volume autre chose que par exemple l'horreur de la forêt,

---

[1] If one keeps on repeating a word to oneself, it soon loses outline and becomes meaningless. Or its normal meaning fades into another—'flower' becomes 'one that flows'. But this is different from looking inwardly at a word while saying it once or twice.

ou le tonnerre muet épars au feuillage: non le bois intrinsèque et dense des arbres.[1]

M. A. G. Lehmann says of the second sentence: "This 'tiers aspect' is, in Mallarmé's terminology and doctrine, the Pure Idea culled from Schopenhauer; in point of fact, though, there is no need to appeal to anything so elusive: if we rid ourselves of such prepossessions, it is clear that the 'tiers aspect' is a new image, a new formal construct."[2]

This is not clear to me; why should Mallarmé use the curious phrase, *fusible et clair,* and speak of the *tiers aspect* being revealed to divination, if he meant by it simply a third image? And why should a third image 'detach itself' from a relation between images?

I think Mallarmé meant something different from an image, but quite simple—the expressive quality of a relationship that is apprehended when two images (verbal or otherwise) are brought into conjunction. If this something were an image, it could be described, but the quality of a relationship can only be inwardly perceived.[3]

In music, for example, an isolated note has no expressive

[1] "Decadent, mystical, the schools that declare themselves or are hastily labelled by our newspapers, adopt as meeting-ground the terms of an Idealism which (parallel with fugues, with sonatas) rejects natural materials and, as brutal, the organising of them by exact thinking: in order to retain nothing but suggestion. To establish between images an exact relationship, so that from it a third aspect, malleable and clear, detaches itself and is revealed to divination. . . . Abolished the pretension, aesthetically an error although it prevails in masterpieces, to inscribe on the subtle paper of the book anything else than, for example, the forest's horror, or the mute scattered thunder of the foliage: not the solid wood intrinsic to the trees."

[2] *The Symbolist Aesthetic in France* (Blackwell, 1950), p. 92

[3] Valéry was always much concerned with relationships. In later life he wrote: "There was a time when I saw (*je voyais*). I saw or wished to see the patterns of relations between things, not the things themselves. *Things* made me smile with pity. Persons who stopped at things were for me no better than idolators. I *knew* that the essential thing was *pattern*." From 'Propos me Concernant', in *Présence de Valéry*, by Berne-Joffroy (Paris: Librairie Plon, 1944), p. 55

significance, though it may have a distinctive character, dependent chiefly on its timbre. But a chord of two notes can be expressive, as in the difference between a major and a minor third. And when notes are related in a time-sequence, they can yield an expressive melody. The musical meaning of a melody remains virtually unaltered at whatever pitch, or on whatever instrument, it is played, showing that it resides essentially in the pattern of relationships between the notes, not in the individual characters of the notes themselves.

With words it is rather the same, but with some obvious differences. An individual word is not void of significance; it has a referential meaning. And words must be used in a time-sequence; there is no verbal equivalent of the musical chord. However, the sounds of words always play into the experience of them, especially (though not only) in poetry. They are a third element, besides the referential and the symbolic meanings, which make up the pattern of relationships that is formed in the reader's mind. Hence to say that 'verbal music' in poetry is irrelevant or unimportant (and this has been said) is as misguided as to treat it as an element on its own, divorced from the other two.

When the sounds of words are cultivated for their own sake, as often in Swinburne, there is a feeling of falling through a gap—the gap left by the poverty or vagueness of significant meaning—into a reverberation of words which are not able to do what actual music can do: communicate symbolically an indefinable experience by their sounds and harmonies alone. Eliot says of Swinburne:

> I am inclined to think that the word 'beauty' is hardly to be used in connexion with Swinburne's verse at all; but in any case the beauty or effect of sound is neither that of music nor that of poetry which can be set to music. . . . What we get in Swinburne is an expression by sound, which could not possibly associate itself with music. For what he gives is not images and ideas and music, it is one thing with a curious mixture of suggestions of all three.

Shall I come, if I swim? wide are the waves, you see;
Shall I come, if I fly, my dear Love, to thee?

This is Campion, and an example of the kind of music that is
not to be found in Swinburne. It is an arrangement and choice
of words which has a sound-value and at the same time a
coherent comprehensible meaning, and the two things—the
musical value and the meaning—are two things, not one.[1]

I am not sure if I follow Mr. Eliot here. If he is saying simply
that poetry needs both musical value and intelligible meaning,
then certainly this is so, but to *separate* the musical value and
the meaning, so that they can be savoured independently of
each other—this, in my experience, cannot be done without
destroying the reader's response to the poetry. Even in very
deliberate examples of sound-effects—

> The moan of doves in immemorial elms
> And murmuring of innumerable bees

—the sounds and meanings of the words are inseparably parts
of the total expressive effect. Tennyson's lines are a little too
obviously contrived, but at least he is keeping his eye on the
object, which is something that Swinburne, as Eliot observes,
often does not: "He uses the most general word, because his
emotion is never particular, never in direct line of vision, never
focused; it is emotion reinforced, not by intensification, but by
expansion."

Let us take a rather less obvious example from Bridges,
where he is speaking of storm-clouds:

> Their shadows fly along the hill
> And o'er the crest mount one by one:
> The whitened planking of the mill
> Is now in shade and now in sun.

The first two lines are pleasant but commonplace; the last two
are much more strongly expressive, partly because they are not

[1] From 'Swinburne as Poet', 1920. Reprinted in Eliot's *Selected Essays*
(Faber, 1932), pp. 310–11

taken from stock, and partly because of the vowel sounds and the beat of the monosyllables in the culminating line. But the vowel sounds are expressive because they strengthen the images which the words evoke. Nor does the monosyllabic rhythm of the last line have a virtue of its own; its virtue is that it reinforces the alternation of sun and shade which the words describe. In poetry it is always the whole pattern, the aesthetic *Gestalt*, that with blended voices speaks. And the effective pattern does not exist on the printed page, but is brought to birth within the apprehending mind.[1]

[1] "All the artist can do is to fashion *some thing* that will produce a certain effect on someone else's mind. There will never be any accurate way of comparing what has happened in the two minds; and moreover, if what has happened in the one were communicated directly to the other, all art would collapse, all the effects of art would disappear. The whole effect of art, the *effort* the author's work demands of the consumer, would be impossible without the interposition, between the author and his audience, of a new and impenetrable element capable of acting upon other men's being. *A creator is one who makes others create.*" From "Reflections on Art", a lecture given by Valéry in 1935. Translated by Ralph Manheim in *Paul Valéry: Aesthetics*, vol. 13 of *The Collected Works of Paul Valéry*, edited by Jackson Mathews (New York, Bollingen Foundation; London, Routledge, 1964), p. 143.

X

A Game of Chess

WHEN I first read of Mallarmé's 'third aspect', disengaging itself from an exact relationship between images, it took me back to an episode during my last year at school. I have never heard of anything quite like it, and it has some bearing on the region behind words. It concerns chess, but to follow it one needs to know only the sort of game chess is, played on a board of black and white squares under rules that determine for each piece its range and power of move.

On a Sunday afternoon in summer I was watching two other boys playing chess in the garden; we were all about eighteen. One of the players, J, was the school champion. I had been urging him to see how far his unconscious mind, if he left it as free as he could, would prompt the best moves. Usually he resisted this, saying he never liked to trust a sudden idea until he had worked it out. But it may have led him to pay more attention to his own mental processes while he was playing.

Presently, on this Sunday afternoon, he began to talk of the pieces as though they had lashing tails. The queen had a long tail; the pawns had very short tails; the knights had crooked tails (they have a crabwise move), and so on. It seemed that he was mentally visualising a piece as a force acting vectorially along the line of its permitted move. He saw it inwardly as a dynamic entity, extending its influence (its 'tail') over whatever squares it commanded at the moment.

That was the first stage. Later on, J began to talk of a pattern of forces—or, more strictly, of a pattern of relations between forces. Imagine all the pieces as forces acting along the lines of their moves. In a given position they will form a network of force-relations. Now forces can be pictured, as lines or rays or 'tails', but a *relation* between forces is a purely abstract concept.

Yet J insisted that what he had before his inner vision, in clear detail, was this purely abstract pattern of force-relations. In order to 'see' it, he said, he had to put his eyes out of focus, until finally he lost sight entirely of the board. The visible set-up was replaced by its abstract counterpart; and by some peculiar, self-hypnotic act of inward concentration J held this relations-pattern before his attention, and was able to study it at leisure.

Further, the pattern revealed to him the state of the game. If he had a strong position, the pattern had for him a look of dominance: the balance of force was on his side. The question he had to study was how to modify the pattern so as to enhance this dominance. Or, if the relations-pattern looked weak, with the dominance against him, how to strengthen it from his own point of view. Having perceived the change required he was at once able—by a process he could never exactly describe—to regain sight of the board and make the corresponding move.

Often the required change stood out clearly, but sometimes it was hard to choose. We asked J which of the two commonest opening moves, P–K4 or P–Q4, seemed to him superior, judged in force-relation terms. He said he could see nothing in it: the resulting patterns were equally satisfactory from the opening player's side.

In the course of one game there was an odd episode when, as soon as J gained sight of the pattern of a certain position, he exclaimed that only a section of the game was in view. To his inner vision it was as though he were looking at a small arena, with blankness where the rest of the pattern would normally have been. This seemed to mean that the point of the game, in that particular position, was concentrated in one part of it; the other pieces were for the moment irrelevant, outside the active pattern of attack and defence.

I doubt if anyone could have inferred this from an ordinary study of the position, and it might have been difficult to establish even by detailed analysis. In this case, of course, we could not prove that J's statement was justified. But it was some evidence, perhaps, that he was not inventing his inner visions.

This disappearance of part of the pattern was too sudden and unexpected.

On another occasion, while he was studying the pattern of a certain position and had thus lost sight of the board, we quietly removed one of the two kings. He seemed not to perceive exactly what we had done—he did not mention the king—but he exclaimed at once that the purpose had somehow gone out of the pattern; had left it aimless, with no point in making any move.

We tried setting up positions from master games, when some player had made a particularly brilliant move, to see whether J could find this move solely by contemplating the pattern, with no preliminary study of the position. Several times he succeeded (and the moves were not easy to find); then we gave him a position which left him in doubt. He could see two likely moves, he said. One was very strong and solid, obviously good. But he preferred the other; it would make the pattern so beautifully 'fragile', equally strong but not so massive —clearly an aesthetic choice.

The first of the two alternative moves was the correct one. The other move looked absurd; but without telling J this we made it, and the obvious reply. He studied the new pattern and gave us a further move, which again pleased him; he said it kept the pattern strong, in the same fragile, fine-drawn way. To us, the move again looked hopeless; without saying so we made it, and again the obvious reply. And now, directly J gained vision of the new pattern, he exclaimed that it had broken down; now it indicated nothing but a lost game.

What had gone wrong? How could bad moves have looked so promising?

On reflection, J said he thought the pattern created by the first of his apparently absurd moves—the pattern that had looked strong but so beautifully fragile—must have had somewhere in it a tiny flaw, a loose link in the relations-pattern, which he had failed to notice. And after his second absurd move, and our reply, the flaw had spread, like a ladder in a stocking.

It had become grossly obvious, and the pattern of his game was seen to be suddenly in ruins.

> Out flew the web and floated wide,
> The mirror cracked from side to side. . . .

From the point of view of his opponent, I suppose, the pattern would have assumed at that moment a look of overwhelming dominance.

Our experiments ended abruptly. While studying relations-patterns J liked to stand up, so as to get a bird's eye view of the board. One day, standing at his shoulder, I saw him sway slightly; next moment he fell back into my arms. He struggled up immediately, crying "I see the move", and reached for the board to make it (it was the right master move), but when he realised what had happened, the experience was a shock; it unnerved him. So much so that for a long time he refused not only to play chess but even to look at a chess position; he was afraid it might entrance him against his will.

His own account of the final episode was that he had been drawn more and more deeply into the relations-pattern, out of himself. He seemed to fear that if this happened again, he might be drawn in still farther and be unable to 'get back'. It was not loss of consciousness that he feared but something more like a loss of personal anchorage—presaged perhaps by his loss of upright balance—if he plunged too far into this region of vividly perceived abstractions. Mallarmé may have experienced a similar fear—"I would have become again the Void".

So our experiments were cut short, but they made a strong impression on me and the other boys who watched them. It seemed to us that anyone able to stand the strain of using regularly this form of inner vision might be able to play perfect chess. He would have to be careful not to overlook tiny flaws in the patterns; granted that, he would always be able to find the best move, without having to reckon ahead. The method could also be used for finding the best line in any opening, without having to work out innumerable variations. If two players both used the method, their games would end always in a draw. Played in this way, chess might become a strict science—and would perish as a game.

It may seem that all this could be easily explained as a piece of make-believe, devised by J to make fools of us. Obviously this cannot be disproved; but knowing J well I could not believe it then and I cannot believe it now. The whole thing, including the final collapse and subsequent anxiety, would have been a remarkably ingenious feat of sustained acting. And if J had been hoaxing us, he would surely have wanted to blow the gaff at some stage in order to enjoy our discomfiture. For him, at any rate, the experience was alarming enough to put him off chess. After leaving school I saw him only occasionally and gradually we lost touch, but I never heard of him playing chess seriously again, though he had shown enough gift for it, even when playing by normal methods, to have gone on to tournament standard if he had wished.

In any event, the existence of a relations-pattern that represents a chess position is not make-believe. A pattern of relations between imaginary forces is what a chess position is. And something like it must arise in the mind when a position is studied. The debatable question is only whether such a relations-pattern can be directly perceived. By a normal player it obviously is not perceived; but if it exists somewhere in his mind, more or less completely, it could have an unconscious influence on his play. Two differences between a good player and an average one may be (*a*) that with the good player the inward pattern is a more nearly complete and accurate representation of the position on the board, and (*b*) that the pattern and its lessons are nearer the threshold of conscious perception, so that he is able to gain more intuitive guidance from it.

A first-rate player will of course need a gift for conscious calculation and evaluation, and generally he will have a wide knowledge of the literature and theory of the game. But positions often occur, especially in the middle game, when it is not possible by 'thinking ahead' to make certain whether one likely move will turn out better than another; the branching variations are too numerous for anyone to work them out completely. In such cases a player may have to rely to some extent on intuition, on the 'look of the board', and a first-rate player may have better intuitions, and so be led to pick the best move more often, because of stronger promptings from the relations-pattern present unconsciously in his mind.[1]

*   *   *

I think there are parallels between J's experience and the experience of words in the mind, but with some obvious differences.

The inner active shape of a word can be mentally perceived; this is the equivalent of inwardly seeing a chess piece as though it had a lashing tail. Anyone who can read has an awareness—an intuitive grasping in Suzanne Langer's sense—of relations between words, or the simplest sentence would be meaningless. Like most people, probably, I am quite unable to visualise inwardly a complete pattern of relations between words; but such a pattern must arise in the mind whenever a sentence is read.

In poetry the pattern becomes more complex, involving the sounds of words and their symbolic meanings, but one may suppose that it *could* be brought before the inner sight of anyone able to perform J's self-hypnotising feat of inward concentration. It would be much richer than a chess relations-pattern, and also (unless a few words were focused in isolation) it would not be static, but changing continually while the poem was heard or read. A wonderful and absorbing 'sight' it might be, as parts of the pattern dissolved and new relations arose in their place, while in the whole was reflected instantly every change in its parts. But to maintain this inner vision while reading or repeating a poem to oneself—this, one may assume, would be even harder than gaining vision of a chess relations-pattern, with

[1] See Appendix

nothing else to do but stare at the static board. Probably the black and white squares helped J to induce the inner vision; whether black and white print could do the same for a reader— I don't know, but it might be more difficult not merely in degree but in kind.

A further difference is that a chess relations-pattern gains its character, its dominance or weakness, from the rules and state of the game. There would be nothing corresponding exactly to this in a verbal relations-pattern; but I think the relations-pattern of a poem would show something like strength or weakness, depending on how far the poem was effectively organised as an expressive verbal instrument.

Would the pattern indicate degrees of aesthetic merit? According to J, a chess pattern was aesthetically attractive when it looked both strong and fragile—a maximum of expression with a minimum of means. Or, one might say, when its form was expressive through and through, as a work of art should be. In poetry this would mean no redundant words, and equally no effort to communicate through the words more than they will bear—no 'emotion slopping about loose'.

The chess equivalent of this latter fault would probably be a deceptive, 'unsound' pattern, promising more than it could achieve. An example of this was the apparently strong position which proved to have barely perceptible flaws, so that after two moves it collapsed. One might call it a sentimental position; it deceived J into liking it—until the unnoticed flaws brought ruin to his game.

A sentimental poem could be regarded in a similar light. A good poem has a firmly-knit structure which exactly fits its content; but if the structure is faulty, with gaps where there should be tensions, then, when the pattern is laid hold of in the reader's mind, it breaks, and the reader falls through it, so to speak, into the mess of residual emotion.

But how can the reader become aware of any emotion not embodied in the words, which are all he has to go by? I think the answer is that the emotion is loosely attached to the words, by implication and association. The words trail it along, but the formal structure does not properly embody it; where it might be, there are gaps.

One might also ask: Since there is no evidence that a verbal relations-pattern ever has been or ever can be directly perceived, in the way J said he perceived the chess pattern, what is the use of trying to compare the two processes?

I think there is an analogy; perhaps this will emerge more clearly if we consider J's performance in connection with some other creative activities of the human mind. If someone has a marked gift for a particular mental pursuit, it means that he can handle easily the relevant concepts; he can hold them clearly before his mental eye and can discern the effect of bringing them into various relationships. Painters can do this with images and colours; mathematicians with symbolical-numerical abstractions; engineers with force-structures, and so on. This is of course not the same as actually 'seeing' a relations-pattern, but the relations-pattern is there in the mind, and its guidance is intuitively apprehended.

Suppose a painter has to decide on the exact shade of colour to use in the course of a partly painted picture. He can mentally visualise various shades, and he needs to discern the effect of placing a given shade in relation to the colours already on the canvas. In his mind there will be a relations-pattern representing the picture so far; he will not be able to 'see' it consciously, but from the effect on the pattern of introducing a new shade of colour he will gain intuitive guidance as to which shade to use. This will correspond to finding the best move in chess, or the right word to complete a line of poetry.

Hence I have found it helpful, in considering how poetry, or any art, *works*, to recall the J episode. It brought out for me the nature of the dynamic pattern of forces which a chess position represents, and showed how this is not simply an idea, but an abstract entity that *can* be perceived. It showed also how the relations-pattern portrays the state and purpose of the game. Underlying a poem (or *mutatis mutandis* any work of art) there is a similar relations-pattern which represents the poet's endeavour to embody in a word-structure the intimations that impelled him to write. When the relations-pattern acts through the words on the reader's mind, a corresponding (though perhaps never identical) relations-pattern is set up in *his* mind, and through it something of the poet's original experience is rekindled in him. It is through a relations-pattern that aesthetic experience is communicated from mind to mind.

★   ★   ★

We can now carry further the question of what poetry is about—what sort of experience it communicates and why this should be valued. This inquiry will lead on to some wider issues: we shall be moving out of the field of literary criticism to consider where poetry and the other arts stand in relation to the accelerating advance of technological civilisation, and what they might contribute to this necessary but hazardous adventure. I want to approach these issues by way of 'nature poetry', its rise and decline and its bearing on our interpretations of the external world.

PART III

THE ARTS IN THE WORLD

XI

Images from Nature

WHEN poetry uses symbolic imagery drawn from the outer world, is it saying anything significant about the world, or does the imagery symbolise only the poet's feelings, his inner life?

Only his feelings, his 'patterns of sentience', most modern critics would say. If poetry seems to make us aware of some aspects of the world that we may not normally perceive, or to bring out some patterns of meaning in its texture—all this is an agreeable illusion. For reliable knowledge about the world we must look to science, not to the charming but deceptive creations of art:

> We may find an image for our own uncircumscribed energies in the sea or the north wind, but we are unlikely to perform sacrifices to Poseidon or Boreas. Sea remains sea for us, and wind remains wind, phenomena of an outside nature, although their mystery and turbulence may make us aware of similar energies in ourselves. Today it is the inward significance which matters, as if the gods had shifted their centre of gravity from the external plain to the inner kingdom of ourselves. That is their true habitat.[1]

This view of nature belongs to our time; it was bound to follow the transition from a participating mode of consciousness to the onlooker mode. In I. A. Richards's early essay, *Science and Poetry*,[2] there is a well-known passage (already mentioned) which in fact describes this transition, though Richards, of course, saw it in a rather different light:

> The central dominant change may be described as the *Neutralisation of Nature*, the transference from the Magical View of the

[1] Thomas Blackburn, *The Price of an Eye* (Longmans, 1961), p. 15
[2] Kegan Paul (Psyche Miniatures series), 1926

world to the scientific. . . . By the Magical View I mean, roughly, the belief in a world of Spirits and Powers which control events, and which can be evoked and, to some extent, controlled themselves by human practices. The beliefs in Inspiration and the beliefs underlying Ritual are representative parts of this view. It has been slowly decaying for some 300 years, but its definite overthrow has taken place only in the last 60. Vestiges and survivals of it prompt and direct a great part of our daily affairs, but it is no longer a world-picture which an informed mind most easily accepts. There is some evidence that Poetry, together with the other Arts, arose with the Magical View. It is a possibility to be seriously considered that Poetry may pass away with it.

In those days Richards believed that the future of poetry depended on poets severing their poetry from any beliefs about the character of the world. "Poetry has constantly the air of making statements, and important statements; which is one reason why some mathematicians cannot read it. They find the alleged statements to be *false*." But if these statements were recognised as pseudo-statements, poets could continue to write in the old way and poetry would continue to have its hygienic effects on the nervous system. "A pseudo-statement", Richards explains, "is a form of words which is justified entirely by its effect in releasing or organising our impulses and attitudes (due regard being had for the better or worse organisations of these *inter se*); a statement, on the other hand, is justified by its truth, i.e. its correspondence, in a highly technical sense, with the fact to which it points."

This recipe for a modern belief-free poetry has not been fruitful; but the picture of nature as 'neutral' is now an accepted commonplace. Hence, if nature appears to have 'moods', they *can* be nothing but projections of human feeling on to a kind of neutral screen.

This view cannot be disproved by a simple appeal to experience, but we should recognise that it does not derive from experience. It is held because it accords with a picture of the world that comes naturally to the onlooker-consciousness; and to accept it involves doing some violence to experience. For even today, when we are all more or less under the influence of the onlooker-consciousness, we do not *experience* nature as neutral, but as hostile or friendly, cheerful or melancholy, turbulent or calm. These are some of nature's 'moods', and in our experience of them there is nothing to suggest that we have put them there. It is true that if we are feeling sad, this may cast a certain greyness over the scene, but that is something we can allow for; we are always still able, if we wish, to distinguish nature's moods from our own.

The onlooker-consciousness, however, is always inclined to analyse an experience into causes and components. If we encounter a radiant spring morning, sunshine and fresh green, we can always say to ourselves that the sun is shining because a ridge of high pressure is crossing the British Isles; the trees are green because the sap has risen and the leaves have broken out of bud, and so on. We can go farther into the biochemistry of plants and the physics of the atmosphere, if we wish. Everything that this kind of analysis reveals is perfectly true and the procedure is necessary for certain purposes, but it carries us away from the direct experience. And although we may seldom engage in it consciously, while out in the country, the knowledge that it can be done, and is the normal scientific approach, sets up a certain habit of mind, suggesting that the direct experience, though agreeable, is somehow superficial or even illusory.

This is rather as though when reading a book we began to consider how paper and ink are made and how printing is done, and allowed these reflections to divert us from actually reading the book and listening to what the author says.

But this simile leaves something out. We are not predisposed by the prestige of science to assume that since we know how a book is made and printed, it can have nothing significant to say; but we are predisposed to the same kind of assumption about the world of nature. We do generally assume that Keats's rainbow can have no 'meaning', since science has explained how this atmospheric phenomenon is produced. When accordingly we come to poetry about nature (and it is the same with all renderings of nature in terms of art), we are inclined to assume that the poem cannot be making us aware of any significance inherent in nature, and therefore can only be telling us something about the poet's feelings.

Of course there are many instances where a poet does use an 'objective correlative' to symbolise human feelings, but why does this method work? Could it work as well as it does unless nature itself were symbolic, capable of speaking a kind of poetic language of its own? Hence it need not be a question of 'either-or'—*either* a projection of the poet's feelings on to a neutral nature, as though on to a blank screen, *or* nature giving symbolic expression to some objectively real characteristics of the universe. When a poet uses images drawn from nature, he may be taking from nature's symbolic language a phrase which also expresses something he has himself felt—something which belongs to his inner life and is not drawn directly from nature, but finds a responsive echo there.

By nature's symbolic language I do not mean a language which can be translated into moral lessons, or into evidence for a wisely beneficent Creator, in the manner cultivated by 18th-century Deists.[1] The 'argument from design' is not worthless, but if we are to derive our conception of the divine from nature as we know it, we have to credit the Deity with attributes that may appear contradictory and are far from wholly beneficent. In any event, this approach to nature is rather like approaching poetry in order to paraphrase it. Since all poetry must have some rational meaning, it can always be paraphrased to some extent, and rational principles can be read out of nature in the same sort of way, as is done by science; but in both cases the symbolic meanings, apprehensible only through direct experience, are set aside.

[1] See Basil Willey, *The Eighteenth Century Background* (Chatto and Windus, 1949), esp. Chapter II, 'The Wisdom of God in the Creation'

We cannot say exactly what are the symbolic meanings inherent in nature's language, but we can say that the experience of them is an experience of something that is akin to ourselves and yet goes beyond our ordinary states of mind. Many people have found there, as Wordsworth did, some kind of untranslatable answer to states of dejection and perplexity—not a final or enduring answer, but one that is felt to have incontestable validity at the time:

> I well remember that those very plumes,
> Those weeds, and the high spear-grass on that wall,
> By mist and silent rain-drops silvered o'er,
> As once I passed, into my heart conveyed
> So still an image of tranquillity,
> So calm and still, and looked so beautiful
> Amid the uneasy thoughts which filled my mind,
> That what we feel of sorrow and despair
> From ruin and from change, and all the grief
> That passing shows of Being leave behind,
> Appeared an idle dream . . . .[1]

Hence the experience of nature's symbolic language runs counter to the view that nature exists merely as an array of phenomena which may be used to symbolise human feelings, but have in fact no meaning for man. This view arose when the old participating consciousness was beginning to wane, and it was necessary for the development of modern physical science.[2] But it has never come naturally to poets and artists. "There is," Mr. Cecil Day Lewis has said, "a most remarkable weight and unanimity of evidence, both in the verse and in the critical writings of English poets, that poetry's truth comes from the

---

[1] *The Excursion*, i, 942

[2] "One usually assumes that the beliefs or unbeliefs of modern man originate in the scientific discoveries made in the seventeenth century; it may be equally correct to say that the scientific discoveries of the seventeenth century could not have been made without the vision of reality, held by man, having undergone a radical change." Erich Heller, *The Disinherited Mind* (Bowes and Bowes, 1952; Penguin, 1961), p. 23

perception of a unity underlying and relating all phenomena, and that poetry's task is the perpetual discovery, through its imaging, metaphor-making faculty, of new relationships within this pattern, and the rediscovery of old ones. . . . It has been my argument throughout that the poetic image, as it wings these higher flights, and searches for connections by the light of an impassioned experience, reveals truth and makes it acceptable to us."[1]

If, however, poets and artists feel bound to adopt the scientific view of nature, then they must decide that nature's symbolic language is only a projection of their own feelings on to the outer world. But they are not bound to adopt the scientific view, for it is only a view, derived not from scientific research but from the limitations of the onlooker-consciousness. And one function of art is to keep alive, during the onlooker-epoch, something of the participating consciousness, so that from this seed may grow whatever new mode of imaginative consciousness may be developed later on. This will restore a communion of man with nature, but in a less instinctive, more active and much more responsible way than was normal or possible in the past. The old participating consciousness was given; the new mode will have to be won.

*   *   *

We are of course often still able, in spite of the waning of instinctive participation, to hear and respond to nature's language with no aid from poetry; but poetry enhances the experience, not only while we are reading it, but also through passages which some aspect of the outer world may bring into the mind. Valéry touched on this in his endeavours to describe the 'poetic state'. I have already quoted one of these accounts;[2] Valéry must have been fairly well satisfied with it, for eleven years later he repeated it in very similar words during the lecture he gave at Oxford in 1939:

[1] *The Poetic Image* (Cape, 1947), p. 34
[2] Above, p. 27

All possible objects of the ordinary world, external or internal, beings, events, feelings, and actions, while keeping their usual appearance, are suddenly placed in an indefinable but wonderfully fitting relationship with the modes of our general sensibility. That is to say that these well-known things and beings —or rather the ideas that represent them—somehow change in value. They attract one another; they are connected in ways quite different from the ordinary; they become (if you will permit the expression) *musicalised*, resonant, and, as it were, harmonically related.[1]

Valéry was probably speaking here not of the outer world itself, but of the outer world presented in a poem and re-created in the reader's mind. But the outer world itself can appear 'musicalised' under the stimulus of aesthetic feeling,[2] or indeed without any such stimulus. This is another way of saying that there are occasions when nature 'speaks', and in a language that is felt to harmonise with "the modes of our general sensibility".

★ ★ ★

In times when a participating consciousness was normal, nature was probably often experienced in ways not very unlike those we call aesthetic or poetic, but with the important difference that they were not consciously noted or named, but taken for granted, and associated not always or entirely with pleasure, but also with feelings of fear and awe. 'Nature poetry' as we know it came into vogue with the Romantic movement, and one of the impulses behind it was a not clearly recognised sense of loss at the waning of the old participating mode. Poets were impelled to seek communion with nature because this was no longer so simple as it once had been.

This wish has led to various sentimental distortions: nature is viewed as innocent and good, in contrast to the wickedness

[1] *A.P.*, p. 59
[2] As in Walter de la Mare's poem, "When music sounds, gone is the earth I know. . . ."

of cities; or as a source of moral edification—'one impulse from a vernal wood'; or nature is humanised, so that the moods of nature are treated not as symbols, but as though nature were actually sympathising with human sorrows and joys. Aldous Huxley has remarked in one of his essays that Wordsworth would have written differently about nature if he had lived in the tropics, where nature is often experienced as inimical to man.

As a result of all this spurious romanticism, 'nature poetry' has become somewhat discredited; and this has reinforced the view that nature is neutral and dumb. However, let us take a familiar short poem, Edward Thomas's *Tall Nettles*:

> Tall nettles cover up, as they have done
> These many springs, the rusty harrow, the plough
> Long worn out, and the roller made of stone:
> Only the elm butt tops the nettles now.
>
> This corner of the farmyard I like most:
> As well as any bloom upon a flower
> I like the dust on the nettles, never lost
> Except to prove the sweetness of a shower.[1]

Evidently, this corner of the farmyard has aroused feeling in the poet, but it is not simply his liking for the place that he is writing about. The lines may have some unknowable root in an emotional tension, possibly connected with dryness and thirst. But it is not exactly a 'pattern of sentience', in Susanne Langer's phrase, that the poem communicates to me. The farmyard spoke to Thomas in a certain way, and through his poem it speaks to the reader, provided the reader's awareness has been heightened by the pattern of the words.[2]

[1] Edward Thomas, *Collected Poems* (Faber)
[2] Similarly of music Stravinsky writes: "A composer's work *is* the embodiment of his feelings and, of course, it may be considered as expressing or symbolising them. . . . More important is the fact that the composition is something entirely new, *beyond* what can be called the composer's feelings." *Expositions and Developments* (Faber, 1962), p. 101

For me, this short poem, fairly typical of Edward Thomas's style, gives some indication that there can be a nature poetry which springs from a valuable aspect of the onlooker-consciousness—its capacity (evident also in modern ecology and ethology) for entering into a relationship with nature which is neither sentimental nor coldly detached. For this relationship to arise, the old participating consciousness had to pass away. But for it to develop fruitfully, it needs to be freed from certain restrictive assumptions bound up with the current scientific world-picture. I call them assumptions because, although they are often supposed to derive from the assured progress of science, they are not scientifically proven or provable; nor do the real achievements of science depend on them. The assumptions most relevant here are these:

1. Matter must ante-date mind, for the earth was in existence as a material entity long before any trace of life—let alone mind—can be found in the geological record.

2. Life arose out of dead matter. Consciousness emerged when living organisms had reached a certain stage of complexity. It is dependent on the bodily organism and must therefore perish when the body dies.

3. The universe is a kind of vast dynamic machine, with no meaning or purpose in any human sense. There may be life, perhaps intelligent life, on other planets somewhere in the galaxy, or beyond it. But these animate beings, if they exist, are in the same situation as our own. They are transient phenomena in a universe wholly indifferent to them.

I believe that most scientists, although they may regard these propositions as almost certainly valid, would agree that they have not been established by scientific research. I am not disputing that natural evolution on Darwinian lines has occurred—the evidence for this is overwhelming—but suggesting that these propositions do not follow inexorably from it, or from astronomical research either.

As regards the first proposition, for example, which may

seem the most obviously plausible of the three, we have to ask what exactly is meant by a material world existing in the absence of mind, for we know of a material world only through mind—through our conscious awareness of its effects on our senses. And what we then experience is not some kind of featureless entity called 'matter', but a rich medley of shapes, colours, scents and sounds. Hence some fairly difficult philosophical problems arise if we try to determine what is meant by a material earth existing prior to mind and therefore deprived of all sense-perceptible qualities, since these can hardly be said to have existence if there is no mind to perceive them.[1]

I shall not now try to explore these philosophical questions; I want only to suggest that the concept of the Earth existing long before mind emerged is not as simple and plausible as it may appear to be at first sight. But I will mention two further points. Our inferences about the early history of the Earth are based on observations made in the present and quite recent past; they involve the assumption that natural processes have always gone on in much the same way and at much the same rate as they are doing now. This may seem a reasonable assumption, but it is an assumption, and a fairly sweeping one. And so is the assumption that because no trace of life is found in the geological record before a certain estimated date, life and mind cannot have then existed in *any* form.

In fact, the propositions listed above (and others could be added) derive from extrapolating certain scientific findings into the unknown. Yet the resulting world-picture forms the half-conscious background of a high proportion of educated opinion today, even among people who know little about science. They assume that we are living in a scientific age and that this kind of world-picture, since it seems to be supported by science, must be largely true. A pervasive climate of thought is created, so that ideas in tune with it are automatically accepted and others rejected; and this has a powerfully imprisoning effect on many minds.

[1] Cf. *Worlds Apart*, by Owen Barfield (Faber, 1963)

I am not saying that the scientific world-picture can be shown to be untrue, or that an alternative picture can be shown to be true; neither demonstration can be effected by scientific methods, or within the limits of the experience normally open to the onlooker-consciousness. Indeed, the scientific picture tends naturally to be accepted because it reflects, and is a product of, the onlooker-consciousness. I am saying only that it should not be assumed to have the authority of experimental science behind it.

Here I am concerned primarily with the influence of this assumption on the arts. If it is taken for granted that poetry cannot reveal anything true and significant about the world, then when poetry (or any art) seems to be speaking of something immanent in the world but not normally apprehensible, this kind of symbolic 'magic' must be sheer illusion, and productive of delusions in those who succumb to it.[1]

Of course, poetry can still be welcomed as a source of pleasure, even if the pleasure may often seem (as it seemed to Valéry) inexplicable. It can still be valued as a means of illuminating and interpreting the inner places, light and dark, of the mind. It can enlarge and enrich our emotional experience by communicating 'patterns of sentience' that are outside the scope of prose. It can freshen and quicken our perceptions of the outer world—but with the proviso here that these aspects of the world are assumed to be symbolic only of human feelings. All

---

[1] Cf. Mrs. Langer's discussion of the aesthetic theory of Otto Baensch, rescued by her from virtual oblivion. She welcomes him as a pioneer who approached her own view of works of art as complex forms which express symbolically the dynamics of human feeling, but Baensch could not get away from what she calls the "slightly mad" notion that the mood of a landscape (I now quote his own words) "appears to us to be objectively given with it as one of its attributes. . . . The landscape does not express the mood, but *has* it. The mood surrounds, fills and permeates it like the light that illumines it, or the odour it exhales." Baensch's essay, first published in German in 1923, is translated in full in the symposium, *Reflections on Art*, ed. Susanne Langer (New York, Oxford University Press, 1961), and is discussed also in Mrs. Langer's *Feeling and Form,* op. cit. (Routledge, 1953)

this, within the framework of the scientific world-picture, poetry can still do. But if the poet is forbidden to interpret the world; if he is held to be incapable of saying anything valid except about the subjective realms of the mind, he will encounter various difficulties.

He may try to have no beliefs, but this prescription has never been found very stimulating, or even feasible. He may take his beliefs from science, in which case he will be what Stephen Spender has called 'inside the cage'.[1] Or he may embrace beliefs that challenge the scientific world-picture; he will then perhaps be respected for his talent, but he will be regarded by the bulk of educated opinion—Richards's 'informed minds' —as a purveyor of myths which are not to be taken very seriously. But there is another danger that affects not only individual poets, but the whole future of poetry. If poetry is confined to subjective realms it can easily be charged with escapism, with cultivating a world of dreams and aesthetic niceties to the neglect of much more urgent and important social and moral tasks. The next step is to contend that the poetic arts should leave their ivory towers or academic groves, stop bemusing people with verbal magic and devote their undeniably persuasive powers to some practically useful end.

This demand, or something rather near it, was made by Richards forty years ago; a similar demand was made in other terms by Matthew Arnold before him; and to today we hear it made in uncompromising terms by the Marxist school. The difference lies in the tasks assigned to poetry—with Arnold, moral education; with Richards, hygienic harmonisation; with Marxists, the inculcation of social awareness and commitment.

[1] "When the poet abandons the belief which connects visible with invisible worlds, he is left with nothing but a problem of adjustment through poetry to the situation of man in the surroundings of alien nature. He is in a cage with bars that are mirrors reflecting only himself, and there is no possibility of entering through the imagination into the factual realities outside." *The Making of a Poem* (Hamish Hamilton, 1955), p. 25

And there are differences also, of course, in the degrees of ruthlessness with which the doctrine is applied.

For a modern example of what the doctrine means in practice, we can turn, not to a dry doctrinaire, but to a man who was a brilliantly original dramatist and something of a poet, and who was led by his gifts into certain conflicts with the Marxism which he always and sincerely professed.

XII

Dramatic Illusion

FOR Bertolt Brecht, the essential function of the theatre was
"to teach the spectator a quite definite practical attitude,
directed towards changing the world".[1] In later life he agreed
that the theatre should also be entertaining, but largely as a
means to the same end. Hence his wish to get rid of dramatic
illusion: the audience should be given no encouragement to
lose themselves in the play. On the contrary, various devices
should be used to hold them at a distance from it (the famous
Verfremdungseffekt), watching it like a spectacle and keeping
alertly awake to its social implications.

Originally, Brecht seems to have meant by the *Verfremdungseffekt* not much more than a 'making strange'—i.e.
presenting a character or an episode in such a way that while
remaining recognisable it would strike the audience with a
shock of surprise. But he believed that this encounter with a
world made strange would arouse in the spectators a wish to
come to grips with it—the opposite of a wish to luxuriate in it.

Brecht's early polemics were directed partly against the
established German theatre of the twenties, with its mixture of
stuffy photographic realism and rhetorical emotion. Here, of
course, he was far from alone: a similar trend away from
representation towards free forms had begun to permeate all
the arts even before the first world war. But he was critical
also of the *avant garde* Berlin producer, Piscator, though in
sympathy with his left-wing politics. Piscator's aim was "to
make a performance at the theatre into one united demonstration of working-class solidarity. Proletarian organisations were
the audience, proletarians the actors, and all were to be welded

[1] *Die Mutter: Anmerkungen* I. Quoted by John Willett, *The Theatre of
Bertolt Brecht* (Methuen, 1960), p. 176

together in a realisation of their common cause."[1] The outcome of all this, Brecht decided, was to give the audience merely an illusion of solidarity; a substitute for the real thing. Having enjoyed a warm feeling of working-class solidarity while in the theatre, they were actually less inclined to strive for it in the harsh world outside. Hence Brecht came to use the *Verfremdungseffekt* as a deliberate technique for keeping the audience detached and awake; of denying them the chance to indulge in debilitating dreams. But he was much too strongly gifted to adhere strictly to his own theories. His best plays owe a good deal of their special character to the tension between his efforts to maintain the *Verfremdungseffekt* and the way in which empathy and dramatic illusion keep on breaking through.

Eventually Brecht came to recognise that empathy could not be altogether kept out; it should be allowed to alternate with detached observation, so as to provide conflicting experiences.[2] But probably there was not much change in the revulsion he had himself always felt at the sight of an audience when sustained dramatic illusion was casting its enervating spell:

> A little massage
> For their flaccid spirits. A little tautening
> Of slackened nerves. Easy adventures, a sense of magic hands
> Bearing them off to a world they cannot master
> And have to give up.[3]

Or again:

> Looking around one discovers more or less motionless bodies
> in a curious state—they seem to be contracting their muscles
> in a strong physical effort, or else to have relaxed them after
> violent strain . . . they have their eyes open, but they don't
> look, they stare . . . they stare at the stage as if *spellbound*,

[1] Ronald Gray, *Brecht* (Oliver and Boyd, 1961), p. 61

[2] '*Unsere eigentliche Bewegung wird durch die Erkennung und Erfühlung des zwiespältigen Vorgangs entstehen.*' From *Schriften zum Theater*, 1957, p. 212

[3] *Gedichte aus dem Messingkauf.* (*Versuche* 14.) Quoted by John Willett, op. cit., p. 169

which is an expression from the Middle Ages, an age of witches and obscurantists.[1]

In himself Brecht was an uneasy combination—a man of strong emotions who was also a determined rationalist. One of his motives for hating dramatic illusion may have been that it involved, he thought, a loss of conscious control—something he always feared in himself. But in relation to his own Marxist philosophy (he was never wholly accepted in Moscow), his attitude was also logical. The only real world, he believed, was the world of daily living, of work and pleasure and struggle and class-conflict and hopes for the future. Therefore, if the theatre appeared to draw people away into some other world, a world of fantasy created on the stage, the experience of it could be nothing but an unhealthy sort of compelled day-dreaming.

What then is the world into which dramatic illusion takes us? Obviously it exists on various levels; on a crude level in the old story of the man who jumped on to the stage during a melo-drama in order to rescue the heroine. Here, dramatic illusion really is compulsive.

On a different level, the level of a play which is true to life and yet has some poetic quality, we are drawn into the action, but we are not prompted to interfere with it, for we are *also* watching it from outside, contemplating it as a work of art brought into being on the stage, through which something true to life, but not manifest in ordinary life, speaks to us. The experience is essentially the same whether we are watching a blank verse drama, or a modern play (a Chekhov play, perhaps) which uses a conventionally realistic setting and ordinary con-versational language. It is an experience, one might say, of life approaching the condition of music. But it is not given by overtly symbolic plays in the Maeterlinck vein; they lack precisely that tension between a rich texture of daily living and something beyond daily living, a music heard through

[1] *Kleines Organon für das Theater* (1948). Quoted by Martin Esslin, *Brecht: a Choice of Evils.* (Eyre and Spottiswoode, 1959), p. 109

the dramatic pattern, which is the essence of poetry in the theatre.

Dramatic illusion is necessary for this experience; but dramatic illusion is only a particularly potent, 'magical' form of the power exercised by the pattern and rhythm of any effective work of art. It is what draws us to participate in the expressive action and purpose of the work.

If someone condemns dramatic illusion as unwholesome, can he stop there? Either he will want to banish the arts from his republic, or he will want to use them for didactic social ends. Here the strict Marxist and the stern religious moralist almost join hands. A young man, a sincere Christian who had rowed for his Oxford college, once said to me (in effect): "Surely the main thing is to do one's duty—to carry out as far as one can the will of God. What has art to do with that—there seems to be no real need for it?" Or again, as old Sir Patrick says to the consumptive young painter in *The Doctor's Dilemma*, "Put down your foolish pencil, man; and think of your condition."

It is quite true that the arts can lead to illusory dreaming; they can provide an excuse for neglecting human and social responsibilities; they can be used to cast glamour over corruption and cruelty. They are a prolific source of temptations and are thus rightly viewed with suspicion by moralists, whether religious or Marxist. But they remain, as they always have been, an indispensable part of human living; and in modern times they have become potentially more dangerous and more valuable—both.

*　　*　　*

How this has happened can be seen by contrasting modern attitudes towards the arts with those found in the aesthetic philosophies of India and the Far East. Here there is no question of the arts throwing a veil of illusion over the real world, since for these philosophies the outer world is itself illusion, *maya*, and the function of art is to pierce the semblance and convey intimations of transcendent realities hidden from ordinary perception. It is not art that deceives, but the world.[1]

The main reason for this contrast, I believe, is that Eastern art (excluding recent responses to Western influence) reflects a mode of consciousness prior to the onlooker mode. Traces of the earlier mode are still evident in European mediaeval art, often concerned not so much with the visible world itself as with using it emblematically to awaken religious feeling or to illustrate religious events. Then, with the onset of the onlooker-consciousness in Europe, the arts come down to earth. Painters set out to explore the outer world; to render it in realistic perspective, to celebrate its glory and its wealth. Writers turn from types and allegories to the drama of individual character and personal feeling. In music, polyphony is followed by the more personally dramatic sonata form, Bach by Beethoven.

From all this the arts gain an immense extension of subjects and resources; an extension paralleled by the discoveries of new lands beyond the seas and by the beginnings of the scientific exploration of nature. Everywhere horizons are falling back; our modern age, reflecting the inquiring onlooker-consciousness, is in course of birth.

All that has been gained in our onlooker-epoch need not be emphasised once more. But it has not been sheer gain. In coming down to earth the arts gave up serenity and entered into a realm of controversy, questioning, doubt. They had to live side by side with the new spirit of analytical science, which likes clear factual prose and does not take readily to poetry. The rift between the 'two cultures' begins here.

At the same time the arts, or some of them, become open to large-scale commercial exploitation and dissemination; today

[1] "Aesthetic experience is a transformation not merely of feeling . . . but equally of understanding. . . . The level of pure aesthetic experience is indeed that of the pure angelic understanding, proper to the Motionless Heaven, Brahmaloka." Ananda K. Coomaraswamy, *The Transformations of Nature in Art* (New York, Dover Publications Inc.; London, Constable, 1956), p. 50

they are in the midst of a rapidly developing technological civilisation which does not quite know what to do with them or what they should do for it. In this situation one of the dangers for the arts is that they will lose their vertical, or transcendent, dimension; and this could happen even while they seemed to be flourishing, more widely cultivated and apparently appreciated than ever before.

This will be apparent if we turn from Brecht to the Austrian poet and critic, Ernst Fischer, also a Marxist, but with unusually wide sympathies. He will lead us towards the general outlook for the arts in the later course of the onlooker-age.

*   *   *

Nobody who reads Fischer's recently translated book, *The Necessity of Art: a Marxist Approach*,[1] can doubt that he is a lover of the arts. He has wide knowledge of the literature and artistic background of countries on both sides of the Iron Curtain. Unlike Brecht, he accepts 'magic' as an essential element in art—not too much of it, but there must be some, or 'art ceases to be art'.

A large part of his book is devoted to tracing the connection of artistic trends and movements with historical phases in the class struggle. Here there are many illuminating points; also many debatable ones. Fischer is anxious not to treat works of art merely as illustrations of a thesis, or to bend them to fit his argument, but I think he sometimes does this all the same.[2]

He goes on to consider the future of the arts in a Socialist society moving towards Communism. He is strongly on the side of the liberalisers and against the doctrinaires; thus he

[1] Pelican Books, 1963

[2] As when he argues that Kafka was concerned *solely* with satirising bureaucracy—a thesis difficult to reconcile with parts of *The Castle*, or with the extraordinary cathedral scene near the end of *The Trial*. Or when he contends that in Beethoven's *Missa Solemnis* there is "not the faintest cloud of the beyond. . . . The 'content' of this mass is not God but man in a revolutionary age."

condemns "the methods of administrative interference in the arts practised during Stalin's lifetime", and adds:

> After the Twentieth Congress, rigid adherence to a 'monolithic' Marxist theory of the arts was no longer obligatory, and although the conservative tendencies are still strong, a variety of different artistic concepts now confront each other within the fundamental framework of Marxism.

In his concluding chapter he debates with an imaginary opponent who says to him:

> "You have said that the mission of art is to help us, half-men that we are, fragmentary, wretched, lonely creatures in a divided, incomprehensible, terrifying class society, towards a fuller, richer, stronger life—to help us, in other words, to be men. But what happens when society is itself the safeguard of a truly human life? All true art has always invoked a humanity that did not yet exist. When once we have attained it, what is the use of all the Faustian magic?"

Fischer replies:

> "The permanent function of art is to re-create *as every individual's experience* the fulness of *all that he is not,* the fulness of humanity at large. . . . Art as the means of man's identification with his fellow-men, nature and the world, as his means of feeling and living together with everything that is and will be, is bound to grow as man himself grows in stature. . . . Not until humanity itself dies will art die."

This power to enlarge and enrich our experience of living in the world is a valuable function of the arts, but their vertical, transcendent dimension (which Marxism naturally cannot admit) is also essential, for it derives not from any mystical doctrine but directly from the way in which aesthetic experience responds to human needs. The arts draw us into the flux of the world and also draw us out of it; they draw us into multitude and also into solitude. We live under the pressure of time, but we also want to gain freedom from time in contemplation. These are all ineradicable human needs, and the arts can help to meet them. But although aesthetic experience has a contemplative character, it differs from those modes of contemplation which lead away from sense-perception into purely inner realms. It is always a contemplation of something perceptible, and of the meaning that is embodied in the perceptible and speaks through its form.

However, any withdrawal from the immediate demands of life and society *can* be viewed as 'escapism', or 'alienation' (a word Fischer often uses). If the 'escape' is into aesthetic contemplation, your view of it will depend on where you consider it leads—into mere dreamy illusion (dramatic or otherwise), or into an experience of something real—not of something quite apart from the world, but of a transcendent dimension which strikes into the world.

It is possible that if in Communist countries the arts are allowed increasing freedom, they will reassert their transcendent dimension; will refuse to recognise as their sole function the enlargement of human experience on the horizontal plane. They may themselves contradict Fischer's assertion that "all that man is not" is simply "the fulness of humanity at large". But it is of course not only in Communist countries that the transcendent dimension is more or less explicitly denied. And the prospect for the arts may depend less on particular ideologies, Marxist or otherwise, than on the pervasive influence of science and technology, which may be more potent than any political creed in shaping the societies of the future.

XIII

Pleasure and Poverty

I T would be rash to prophesy how science and technology will
affect the arts in the long run, but some current trends can be
discerned. Their most evident direct bearing is not so much on
recognised artistic activities, or on aesthetic experience in the
full sense, as on something simpler that might be called aesthetic
pleasure in daily life.

This kind of pleasure may spring from a relationship between
a person and his surroundings, or from his relation to the work
he is doing, where this is concerned with shaping and giving
form. It has generally been much more widely enjoyed than
the pleasures given by actual works of art. It is peculiarly
satisfying, for unlike some pleasures it does not stir up a restless
desire for more, and a life without it is poor. But the sources of
it are becoming scarcer in the modern world. Aesthetically
agreeable surroundings are very often destroyed by development schemes and expansions of industry—though these *can*
achieve artistic merit in new forms—and aesthetically satisfying
work is constantly threatened by mechanisation and mass-
production.

For example, to plough a field with horses can yield considerable aesthetic pleasure (though the ploughman might not
give it that name, or any name). To plough with a tractor can
yield some aesthetic pleasure, but less, partly because it requires
less skill and partly because contact with the earth, the part of
the world that is being shaped, is less direct. In time we shall no
doubt reach the next stage: the tractor will need only occasional
radio signals to keep it under control. The operator (hardly still
a ploughman) will merely turn a dial and press a button now
and then. He might be able to do it while sitting at home and
watching the field on a television screen. He might prefer this to

driving a tractor, especially in winter, but he would not get much aesthetic pleasure from the work.

Many labour-saving devices have this effect: they come between the human being and the work. I am not at all saying they should be abandoned: only that the loss in terms of aesthetic satisfaction should be recognised.

This is not because machines are inherently hostile to aesthetic pleasure. A skilled craftsman can get a great deal of aesthetic pleasure from working with his lathe. But the tendency always is for these skilled manual craftsmen to be needed in smaller numbers. New machines, more nearly automatic, are devised. The machine-craftsman becomes a machine-minder, or an operative on a production-line. Production rises: satisfaction is lost.

★   ★   ★

We have moved into a world where technology will be increasingly in demand: for coping with mass poverty and rising populations in some countries, for raising living standards and extending 'affluence' in others. But there is a sense in which the old phrase, "starving in the midst of plenty", could apply particularly to an affluent country, if the tendencies inherent in technology were carried to an overriding extreme. One can imagine a society in which there really was no oppressive poverty; where high levels of health and hygiene were taken for granted; where streamlined efficiency prevailed and even the traffic problem had been solved—and where, all the same, the actual experience of living would suffer from the bleakness of the environment and the mechanised character of the daily round. No-one would be poor, but everyone would be poor.

This is a not unfamiliar picture, of course; tendencies in this direction are already evident in most modern countries. They can be alleviated but are not likely to be altogether reversed. It seems to be part of the human lot to explore the fields of technology and to gain increasing control over nature, in spite of the various hazards involved. Or it will be agreed, at any rate, that the affluent countries will want more affluence, and that they are committed to the enterprise of helping the under-developed countries to achieve something like Western standards of civilisation, as these countries are themselves bent on doing—again in spite of the hazards involved. All such endeavours may be defeated by weight of numbers, if populations continue to rise unchecked; but for making the endeavour technology is an essential instrument. We must therefore expect social life to be increasingly shaped and stamped by science and technology; with the result that people will come to be spared a great deal of brutish toil, while at the same time a great deal of the satisfaction that used to come from the exercise of craft skills will be ruled out. Hence in a technological civilisation there should be more need, not less, for the arts—both for the practice of amateur arts and for professional performances made widely available. They will be needed as sources of refreshment in the dry land.

In fact, there is evidence to show that something like this is already happening. Never has so much good music been heard by so many. Some art exhibitions are crowded to queuing point; amateur painting groups and summer schools multiply; there is a steady sale for expensive art books. Poetry (Betjeman apart) is seldom profitable, but a Poetry Book Society keeps going; poetry festivals are held in London theatres. The B.B.C. and I.T.V. are powerful new sources of patronage.

All this could indicate that the arts are doing very well in face of advancing technology—or because of it. People may be turning to the arts precisely because other aspects of modern life are unsatisfying. But I am not sure if the outlook for the arts is altogether as promising as this evidence might suggest. I am here concerned particularly with the outlook for poetry, the most 'useless' of the arts, but one cannot treat poetry as an entirely special case. Its future is bound to be influenced by the general place and valuation of the arts in society, and some of the latest tendencies in the other arts can raise doubts as to what this place will be. Obscure, harsh, hideous, meaningless—epithets of this kind have often been launched at new artistic trends which eventually came to be accepted; but the *avant garde* trends of today, especially in music, painting and sculpture, seem to signalise a radical break with tradition for which there is perhaps no precedent in the past. It seems a question whether forms of art which are determined to offer so little pleasure to the senses will ever achieve more than a specialised appeal.

In any event, it would be useless to deplore these tendencies; they would not occur if they were not impelled by a current wider and deeper than themselves. I think this is the same current that has produced Existentialism, as a philosophy very typical of the onlooker-consciousness at its present stage. In order to reach some understanding of modern artistic trends, and also of some associated trends in religion, we must enter a little way into the mood of Existentialism. This will seem to take us rather far from the arts, but we shall return with a clearer view of them.

XIV

Age of Anxiety

ANY attempt to characterise briefly a philosophy whose pantheon includes figures so diverse as Kierkegaard, Heidegger, Jaspers, Sartre and Gabriel Marcel will have to leave out a lot. But it seems roughly accurate to say that in Existentialism we can discern three strands of revolt. Its best-known aphorism is "Existence precedes essence"—i.e. the primary human experience is of living, not of thinking. The Existentialist does not say "I think, therefore I am", but "I am because I live"—because of what I directly experience as a living, striving, suffering mortal man. Existentialism does not despise the achievements of human reason; what it attacks is the exaltation of abstract reasoning as the essential or most 'real' activity of man. It calls to the aviators of philosophy, from Plato onwards to Hegel: "You still have to *live* on the ground."

Secondly, since living is always an individual experience, Existentialism is in revolt against all those modern tendencies which treat persons as units in a mass. It is a revolt against de-personalisation. Thirdly, it is a revolt against the liberal optimism which holds that social reforms and scientific progress can in time make men happy and contented; can remove the tragic, doomed element from human life. For to suppose this is to ignore and repress an unalterable part of the human situation; it is an attempt to get rid of the Furies by not looking at them, which means that they will return all the more destructively through being able to take the liberal optimists unawares—as the Nazi furies did.

Existentialist man is sure only that he exists; that he cannot escape the responsibility for choosing how, in what posture, he is going to live; and that he will die. He has been driven to this bleak outlook because the old religious securities that nursed him, made the world a place where he could feel cared for and at home, have been destroyed by advancing science; he feels that he is standing alone and naked in face of a meaningless and pitiless universe. Thus he finds no comfort in the world and is driven back on himself; but he finds no reassurance, no security, there either; within himself he encounters his own conflicts and insatiable desires.

I call Existentialism a typical philosophy of the onlooker-epoch at its present stage because the existentialist picture of the world is very like the picture that the pure onlooker-consciousness will always tend to reach. But the mark of existentialist man is that while he seldom questions this picture—does not ask whether it may not be a projection of a limited phase of human consciousness on to the world outside—he does not calmly or stoically accept it, as a scientific humanist might do. He adopts a stance of defiance towards it and asserts that with this gesture he proves and experiences his freedom as a living, existential man.

★   ★   ★

What has this to do with modern art? The tendency of modern art, also, is to turn away from interpreting the outer world and to draw its subject-matter from within. Just as the discovery of perspective marked a going out of art into the world, a confident exploration and enjoyment of it, so the abandonment of perspective by Cubism and abstract art—a development parallel so the abandonment of musical 'perspective', tonality, by contemporary composers—marks a turning inwards. But by turning inwards towards his own unconscious the artist does not find harmony but conflict; not order, but a chaotic interplay of urges and desires. The resulting works may indicate an endeavour to find refuge in the cool impersonality of abstract designs, or a wish to express (and so perhaps to relieve) the tensions and disorders within. And the artist may feel that he is thus also responding to and expressing the conflicts of an unpeaceful world. "The subjectivity that is generally present in modern art is a psychological compensation for, sometimes a violent revolt against, the gigantic externalisation of life within modern society. The world pictured by the modern artist is, like the world meditated upon by the existentialist philosopher, a world where man is a stranger."[1]

In modern literature we have seen a similar breaking down of traditional order; a movement towards free, disjointed rhythms and (in prose fiction) towards fluid impressions instead of logical narrative; and a similar search for material in the unconscious sources of the mind. "If we think, for example, of Manet, Mallarmé, Joyce or Stravinsky", writes Professor Edgar Wind, "it would seem that almost all the artistic triumphs of the last hundred years were in the first instance triumphs of disruption: the greatness of an artist became manifest in his power to break up our perceptual habits and disclose new ranges of sensibility."[2] These trends spring from the same roots as Existentialism, but of course they go much farther back—writers were beginning to recognise and explore the unconscious from the early days of Romanticism onwards, long before Freud.[3]

*   *   *

There are parallels to Existentialism also in the religious field: the same turning away from abstract formulations towards immediate experience. One example of this (already touched on) is a new interest in mysticism, both Eastern and Western, evident in the number of relevant books, including a Pelican anthology,[4] which have come out during the last few years. Another example (and here Existentialism has been a direct influence) is the view now widely advanced—notably by

[1] William Barrett, *Irrational Man,* op. cit., p. 43

[2] *Art and Anarchy* (Faber, 1963), p. 18

[3] See L. L. Whyte, *The Unconscious before Freud* (New York, Anchor Books, 1962)

[4] F. C. Happold, *Mysticism: A Study and an Anthology* (Pelican Books, 1963)

Professor John Macmurray—that the essence of religion lies in the experience of personal relationships, the 'I and thou'. Finally, there is the wide response aroused by the Bishop of Woolwich's best-selling paperback, *Honest to God*,[1] where the emphasis is on inwardness and 'depth', as opposed to the traditional idea of looking for God in Heaven, or somewhere 'above', and where, again, personal relationships are said to be the heart of all true religion.

It seems certain that in *most* ways religion stands to gain from these trends. Beliefs accepted on authority belong to a pre-scientific age; in fact, onlooker man cannot properly speak of 'believing', except colloquially. He needs to know, and nothing important can be known in the religious realm except through personal experience. But if it is argued that a way towards the Divine is to be found *only* through inward mysticism, or *only* through personal relationships, or only in 'depth' and never 'out there' in space, then I think the gain in one dimension, so to speak, will be accompanied by a loss in others.

This is a loss to which onlooker man is in any case exposed. By losing the capacity to see nature as expressive, and by acquiring the capacity to observe nature with detached objectivity, he was enabled to embark on the process of measuring, analysing and experimenting which led to modern science. This was a necessary development, but still it involved a loss; a loss to be reckoned in with the great gains—so much more obvious than the loss—which science has brought to mankind. It is largely because of the loss that a reckless and insensitive exploitation of the earth and its resources, including its wild life, has occurred. And what is the prospect if Western religion is now to be heard saying through its most currently influential voices that onlooker man, after all, is right—no transcendent element is to be found in nature, no signature of the Divine; all that is illusion and superstition; *only* through inward experience and personal relationships does God speak to man?

To put this in an over-simplified picture, I see on the one

[1] S.C.M. Press, 1963

hand a genuine deepening of religious experience for many people; a very necessary getting away from literalism and crude anthropomorphism—the 'Old Man in the sky'—in the interpretation of religious language; a going out of religion into the common life and fellowship of men. I see all this as a most real gain. But on the other hand I see our planet, the earth and all the realms of nature, and the cosmic spaces, the entire external world—all this I see as thrust out from religious reference, denied any sacramental approach, abandoned to the mercies of a science which treats it simply as something to be analysed and brought into subjection; as material to be *used* for extending human command and multiplying human wealth. In a still simpler and cruder picture, I see people genuinely finding a way towards the Divine in their own lives and the communion of friends; but around them I see a wilderness, glittering with the constructions of technology, where no living water flows.

"For the invisible things of Him since the creation of the world are clearly seen, being perceived through the things that are made, even His everlasting power and divinity."[1] This has now to be denied.

*　　*　　*

Many books will probably be written on the rather new approach to religion which the Bishop of Woolwich (drawing on and quoting from a number of other writers, especially Tillich and Bonhoeffer) has introduced to a wide public. Here I want only to touch on a few points; they have some bearing on the future of the arts.

We are told that 'supranaturalist' views of the world are unacceptable to modern man; they are childish, pre-scientific. Under this condemnation come any notions that there may be other worlds or realms transcending or interpenetrating the world we normally perceive, together with any religious

[1] Romans, I, 20

doctrines which appear to depend on such notions. God is neither 'up above' nor 'out there'.[1]

It is quite true that notions of this kind are foreign to most people today. They do appear to belong to a pre-scientific age. But this is not because science has disproved them. It is because they are foreign to the onlooker-consciousness. But it is arbitrary to assume that the world revealed to our normal sense-perceptions—the only world open to the onlooker-consciousness—is the only world or realm that can exist.

This assumption derives from another assumption, equally arbitrary—an assumption which lies at the root of everything written by the opponents of 'supranaturalism'. They assume that the onlooker mode of consciousness is the only valid mode and its report on the outer world the only true report. The possibility that this mode has evolved from other modes and will probably evolve further, with each mode giving a different and partially valid picture of the world, is not reckoned with. This is a modern equivalent of the mediaeval conviction that the earth was the unique centre of the universe.

*   *   *

Now as to personal relationships. The onlooker-consciousness makes a person more aware of himself; it enhances self-consciousness. Hence it fosters the illusions and the destructiveness of egoistic individualism, sufficiently evident in the modern world. But it leads also to a keener awareness of other people as persons. The uniforms of class and rank, which protected people from having to meet as persons and provided an accepted code of behaviour for most occasions, are no longer comfortable. Even where they are still worn—as the uniform of colour still has to be—the person inside is now expecting to be seen.

[1] The word 'supranaturalist' conceals several assumptions: that a natural order exists 'out there', independently of our sense-perceptions; that it has a definable boundary, and that we know where the boundary is. See Owen Barfield, *Saving the Appearances* (Faber, 1957)

In apparent contradiction to this tendency, certainly, are the de-personalising tendencies which arise in the modern world from sheer numbers and statistics and the desire for efficient organisation. This treatment of people as units, items in a survey or a plan, is not entirely avoidable in crowded societies, but it can also be cultivated as a means of not having to cope with the irritating varieties of individual human needs. Yet the needs are at least recognised; hence the humanitarian-welfare movements which are also characteristic of our modern time.

I think the underlying trend towards the shedding of uniforms and the meeting of persons as persons will continue, with the effect of making personal relationships both more difficult (as in marriage) and potentially more rewarding than they were in the hierarchical past. Hence it is not surprising that onlooker man, unable to discern any meaning in the outer world, should turn to personal relationships for his religion. And up to a point he is justified. I believe that for most people the quality of their personal relationships is more important, of more enduring value and significance, than anything else they may achieve in life, however outwardly successful they may be. What I do not believe is that personal relationships are the *only* relations of communion to which human beings are called. A human being is the nexus of many relationships; he is consciously aware of only a few of them. A Christian might think of the communion of angels, or of the communion of saints, or of the communion between living and dead. But let us think only of the Eucharist. Here are persons gathered together in communion, but not only with one another. They are in communion also with the bread and the wine, fruits of the earth. The substance of the earth, of the created outer world, enters into this sacrament.

If one were to say that the dimension of transcendence strikes in always through *relationships*, I think it would be true. But it would be true not only of many forms of communion; it would be true also of works of art. For the essence of a work of art is

134

that some elements from the outer world are brought into an operative and expressive relationship with one another.

*   *   *

Now we will return to the outlook for the arts. The relevant connection is that under the hand of the artist, or through his words, the world appears to us in a different light; it seems to be transfigured, to acquire a dimension of depth, to speak and to have meaning. But if it is held that the world *cannot* have meaning, then it must also be held (and it is generally held nowadays) that the arts have nothing valid to say about the world, but can communicate only 'patterns of sentience'; these are projected on to the outer world, endowing it with illusory significance. This view of the arts must limit *their* significance; must restrict and impoverish what they could do for us, and for our technological civilisation.

*   *   *

Let us think of the commonest modern ailment, anxiety.[1] It has manifold causes. There are the familiar anxieties about livelihood and status and 'keeping up with the Joneses'; and the anxieties about 'where is science taking us' and the threat of nuclear war. People in modern industrial societies are committed to a regime of continuous competitive change, but they are not adapted to it—not adapted to living always in a long-distance express train bound for an uncertain destination; theoretically a one-class train, but with a struggle for the first-class seats always going on.

Most of these anxieties—we may suppose—could be remedied by improvements in the handling of social and

---

[1] "The secret of happiness lies in the avoidance of Angst (anxiety, spleen, noia, guilt, fear, remorse, cafard). . . . We know very little about Angst, which may even proceed from birth trauma, or be a primitive version of the sense of original sin, but we can try to find out what makes it worse." Palinurus, *The Unquiet Grave* (Hamish Hamilton, 1945), p. 22

economic affairs. But there is a basic modern anxiety which cannot be relieved in that way. This is the anxiety that arises (or it may remain half-conscious or unconscious) from the ego feeling itself alone in an unfriendly universe; alone no less in crowds, or even sometimes among friends, with glass walls between. These are marks of the onlooker-age, an age of anxiety from the first. The ego is thrust back on itself, deprived of the reassurances that were open to it in the ages of faith, inherently given to doubt; existentially certain only of its own isolation and of advancing death.

I am far from saying that the arts could cure this kind of anxiety, but—given certain conditions—I think they could alleviate it. For the arts seem to tell us that the world is not alien and indifferent to man, but has a meaning and purpose which are in some way relevant to human life. They do not speak only of beauty and serenity in the world, or there would be no tragic art, but they seem to tell us that tragedy is not blind waste.

The crucial word is *seem*. If the arts are regarded as capable of communicating only 'patterns of sentience', they can have nothing valid to say about the world. But if it were accepted that what they say need not be an illusion, then they could communicate some confidence in the world; some confidence that the world is not only what it appears to be, and especially not only what it appears to be when viewed through the restricted aperture of the onlooker-consciousness.[1]

The implication of this is that if the arts are to bring an effective counter-influence to the de-humanising and anxiety-promoting tendencies of our technological civilisation, they need the background of a world-picture which is *open* to a religious interpretation. Given that, an agnostic would have no difficulty with the arts on this score. He could recognise through

[1] We have only Elizabeth Brentano's word for it that Beethoven said to her of his music: "Those who understand it must be freed from all the miseries which the others drag about with themselves." But it seems not very likely that her report (in a letter to Goethe) was a complete invention.

his own experience that the arts speak of the world as having meaning; he would not have to associate the experience with any religious creed. But anyone who takes it for granted, as scientifically established, that the world has no meaning and cannot have one, will have difficulty with the arts, if they act on him as more than casual entertainment. When they appear to speak of meaning in the world, he will have to treat this as an illusion and interpret the experience in some other terms. He may accept it simply as a private aesthetic pleasure (as Valéry did), or he may feel (as Brecht felt) that illusions are unhealthy and that the undoubted persuasive power of the arts should be harnessed to some practical social end.

The impulse to write poetry seems to be enduring; poetry will no doubt continue to be fairly widely written and less widely read. But already most modern societies could do without poetry and hardly notice it. One can imagine a future in which the only widely recognised functions for the arts—outside small aesthetic coteries—would be either to provide entertainment, stimulating or tranquillising, or to serve as media for publicity and propaganda. And this would happen not only because of commercial pressures, but also because in a prevailingly secular climate it would be hard to find any good reason why the arts should be supposed to have any other significance.[1]

* * *

[1] "My own view is that we are moving away in England from the traditional liberal culture, centred on literature, to a new and less liberal and more descriptive kind of culture based not on science, which is specialist, but on sociology. . . . Sociology is one of the most pervasive subjects within the university, and one of the most popular. Sociology . . . is even practised by the novel, which now tends to be descriptive and provincial, not concerned to chart the international modern mind but simply to show social progress, often from the point of view of the under-privileged. The kind of writer who is committed to an ideal of civilization seems to give way to the anti-cultural writer, the writer who, in fact, sees no use for art." Malcolm Bradbury, 'Literary Culture in England Today'; *The Listener*, 9.8.62.

If the arts need something like a religious background, does it follow that religion needs the arts? There have been two contrasting attitudes about this—*for* the arts as aids to ritual and devotion, and as a means of symbolically expressing religious truths; and *against* the arts as seducers from the strict path of moral duty and the salvation of souls. Both attitudes, I think, are justified, but neither is justified alone.

The second attitude is heard first in the Old Testament, as an innovation so strange and exacting that the Hebrews were constantly backsliding from it. "Thou shalt not make unto thee any graven image. . . ."

This austere note is heard again at intervals in Christian times, but not strongly in Western Europe until after the Reformation. Then there is again a casting out of images and a stern insistence that nothing in the world must distract a man from the naked encounter with God in his own soul.

A harsh and barbarous-sounding command; but it can be understood in the light of the transition from participating forms of consciousness to the onlooker mode (of which the ancient Hebrews were in a particular sense the precursors). For the onlooker-consciousness in its religious aspect is compelled by its loss of participation to look for the Divine within; only there, at first, can it be found. This trend is strongly evident today, as we have seen; a religion based on personal relationships and 'depth' will have little need for the arts, except as an occasional source of pleasure and refreshment, quite distinct from their main purpose.

But the casting out of images represents a transitional stage, not a final one. Those who treat it as final—as a final and wholly beneficial growing out of a mythological world-picture—will not only continue to have no great need or use for the arts, but will continue to regard the outer world as a place divorced from religious concern.

The onlooker-epoch will not last for ever; the evolution of consciousness will go on. But the religious world-picture will not return in its old form. In that form it was, as it were, given to man; in this sense it does belong to his childhood. In his adolescence he loses it, and with adolescent confidence feels sure it was altogether childish and that to be free of it is sheer gain. But when he grows out of adolescence he will be able to create a world-picture such that he will experience the Divine in the depths and in the heights, with a new and more immediate understanding of the old Hermetic saying, 'As above, so below.' During adolescence he reverses the saying into 'As below, so above', and interprets the 'above' as an illusory projection from below.

XV

Down to Earth

TECHNOLOGY brings some dangers for the arts, but also opportunities: architecture, engineering, industrial design are obvious examples. And it is the productions of technology, rather than works of art in the traditional sense, which will increasingly set their stamp on the visible civilisations of the future, and on the face of the earth itself.

This means that a vast new realm of human freedom is opening up. In the past, men had neither the knowledge nor the power to take hold of more than a few natural substances and remodel them in accordance with their own demands and desires. As cultivators they had to follow nature; in building and making things they were limited by the materials they could get and handle. But now, with the application of modern science to the earth and its resources, they are coming to be almost as free in moulding their environment as in creating works of studio art.

The idea that they ought to use this potent new freedom responsibly is familiar; it grows banal with repetition. They ought not to let cities sprawl into subtopias, or turn fertile lands into dustbowls, or destroy landscapes for convenience, or wipe out whole species of animals and so on. But to what or whom is their responsibility due?

The usual answers are 'to mankind', or 'to posterity'. But to regard these responsibilities as the *only* ones may be wrong; parochially wrong, perhaps.

The kingdoms of nature are bound to be in some sense under the authority of man. He lives among them, the only creature capable of looking before and after, of making plans in accordance with a conscious choice. Only by living at the most primitive food-gathering level could he leave the kingdoms of nature alone. But science has now given him an altogether new power over them; and what he makes of them may be of more than human concern.

This idea runs counter to the current scientific world-picture, but perhaps Blake indicates it:

Eternity is in love with the productions of time

One could feel, looking round at the world and back over history, that Eternity must be easily pleased; but Blake was very far from being pleased with all he saw around him. Yet he held that the productions of time, which must include the artefacts of man, have a more than transient significance; they do not exist for the pleasure or displeasure of man alone. How he shapes the world now under his power will be of concern also to the eternal Powers from whom the first creation sprang.

In earlier chapters I was considering works of art mainly in terms of human response. But a work of art exists also on its own account; it is a piece of the world refashioned into an aesthetic form. A poem once written down is a piece of the world—the world of language—although it resembles music in being imperceptible until it is heard or read. Thus one might say that a work of art gives a semblance of eternity to a piece of the world.[1]

Of course, semblances of eternity are manifest also in the world of nature, but there they are fragmentary, often fleeting or overlaid with nature's profusion, caught into the struggle and tumult of abounding life. In works of art they are given a more expressive and enduring form.

---

[1] In a lecture to the Goethe Society in Vienna (1888), Rudolf Steiner once said, referring to a passage in *Faust*: "It is clearly stated what art stands for. Not for the embodiment of the supersensible, but for the transformation of the physical and actual." In a note to the printed text he added: "In art, physical reality is transfigured through its appearance as though it were spirit. To this extent, artistic creation is not an imitation of anything already in existence, but a continuation, springing from the human soul, of the cosmic process."

Every human artefact can perhaps be regarded either as a work of art, or as neutral, or as a work of anti-art. It would seem reasonable to put the great majority of artefacts into the neutral class, but I am not sure. We are beginning to learn something—not yet very much—about the powers of form. A small change in molecular pattern can turn a harmless substance into a toxic one, although the elements composing it are unaltered. When we twist the tuning knob of a radio set, we are changing the form (and so the resonance) of the condenser plates by moving one plate in relation to the other. There is no change of substance, but the change of form cuts out one programme and brings in another.

Hence it may be that the form given to any human construction does matter in ways not to be judged solely in terms of functional efficiency and convenience. Artefacts shaped with no artistic feeling (which is not opposed to functional efficiency but goes beyond it) should probably be ranked as works of anti-art, and they may have, but in reverse, some of the potency of works of art. They may resonate in tune with some dehumanising influences and so give them entry into human life.

Modern civilisation is committed to living on the technological level; but it will be possible to infuse this with spiritual values—religious, aesthetic and scientific—and so with the nourishment that human beings need.[1] Or it will be possible to live only on the technological level, which would mean living in a spiritual desert, however high a standard of prosperity and comfort might be achieved.

In thinking of the future of the earth, we have to reckon with very long periods; even a nuclear war would probably leave parts of the world habitable and life would go on. We

[1] By scientific values I mean those expressed in exact observation, respect for facts and the patient, impartial search for knowledge. In a technological civilisation these values are not likely to be ignored, but they can offer spiritual nourishment only in so far as the search for knowledge is not distorted by subordination to a search for power.

may expect that new forms of civilisation and new modes of consciousness will arise, different from ours in ways we cannot now imagine. But the responsibility of human beings for the province of earth will remain, through all cycles of time to come.

THE CEMETERY BY THE SEA

A rendering of Paul Valéry's *Le Cimetière Marin*

This quiet roof, white-flecked with doves,
Gleams through the pines, beyond the graves:
The sea, the sea, its ever-reborn waves
Composed in peace by noon's impartial fire!
Here is reward for thought, to pause and look
At where the gods have passed beyond desire.

See how the sun's quick-weaving artifice
Consumes the diamond foam: a scene as though
Conceived by peace itself. And when the sun
Rests on the western steep—pure images
From the eternal fount—then time in flow
Receives their radiance; dream and truth are one.

Minerva's temple, calm and reticent,
Enduring treasure; here the sea's proud gaze,
Sleepy beneath its fiery surface-haze,
Speaks to my silence. Born within the soul
This temple rises; but its eaves are gold,
Its thousand tiles a thousand lustres hold.

Temple of time, whose tribute is a sigh,
Climbing to this pure spot, I come to know
How well its sea-horizon stretched below;
And like my final offering to the gods,
The careless serene brilliance seems to sow
Over the height its sovereign disdain.

As the sweet fruit in tasting melts away,
Its very absence turning to delight

Within the mouth, so here I breathe the day
When I like fume of smoke shall be no more,
While to the consumed soul the vibrant sky
Sings of the murmuring wave along the shore.

Fair sky and faithful, see the change in me,
After these years of pride and idleness
And yet of power, to this bright wilderness
I give myself; the houses of the dead
Are shaded by my moving shadow and
I learn acceptance of its fleeting tread.

My soul laid open to the solstice fire,
Light's admirable justice I embrace,
Her pitiless weapons. To your primal place
See, I restore you. But this tribute paid,
Light given back her purity must leave
A second half of melancholy shade.

O for myself, within myself alone,
Where near the heart a poem has its ground,
Between the nothing and the pure event
I wait to hear my hidden greatness sound;
But in the soul this cavernous bitter well
Has only empty echoes to foretell.

Pretended prisoner in this leafy maze,
Consuming the frail foliage with your fire,
Dazzling your secrets on my shuttered gaze,
What body drags me to this idle end
Or brow attracts me to this place of bones?
A spark engendering thought of absent ones.

Sacred precinct, bathed in immaterial fire,
The earth to light makes offering in return;
Here I find pleasure, where the torches burn:

Gold and stone and sombre cypress-tree,
Marbles trembling under veils of shade,
And sleeping by my tombs, the faithful sea.

And you, resplendent watchdog, keep, O keep
The idolater from my solitude!
With shepherd's smile I graze my peaceful sheep,
These tombs, mysterious flock. Away from me
O keep the prudent doves, the visiting gleam
Of curious angels, and the useless dream.

Once here, the future turns to idleness.
The dry heat scored with grating insect-whirr;
All is dissolved in burning air and changed
Into I know not what strange elixir.
Life stretches vastly, drunk with emptiness,
The mind is clear, and sweet is bitterness.

Well off the dead, warm now in earthy dress,
The earth which parches up their mystery.
High noon above, noon standing motionless,
Conceives itself, content with its own range,
Crowned with perfection, head and diadem:
I am the ferment of your secret change!

Through me alone your fears are held in bond;
My doubts, repentances, compulsions are
The only flaw in your great diamond. . . .
But in the marble-heavy night,
Among the tree-roots, a vague populace
Has turned towards you slowly, out of sight.

They have dissolved into a thick absence,
Red clay has drunk the whiteness of the creature,
The gift of life has gone into the grasses;
Where is each personal art and private feature,

The souls who spoke with old familiar phrases?
Where tears would tremble, now the fine worm
   passes.

The high sharp cries of tickled girls,
Eyes under moist lids, the teeth like pearls,
The charming breast where danger lingers,
The blood that glistens when the lips give way,
The final gifts and the defensive fingers—
It all goes back to earth, back into play!

And you, grand soul, what is it that you crave?
A dream devoid of those false flattering hues
Conjured by mortal eyes from gold and wave?
Will you still sing when by the air possessed?
Come, nothing endures! A ghost is all I am!
Holy impatience dies with all the rest.

Meagre this gilded immortality,
Terribly laurelled, feigning to give rest,
Making of death a mother's gentle breast:
A lovely lie, the piety wearing thin!
Who does not know and who does not refuse
This empty skull and that eternal grin?

Fathers profound, your heads untenanted,
Under so many shovel-loads your bed,
Yet in the earth you echo where we tread.
The urgent worm that plies around the bone
Is not for you, asleep beneath the stone:
It lives on life—on mine, on mine instead!

Love is it, perhaps, or hatred of myself?
His secret tooth gnaws in so close to me
That any name would do. No matter, he
Sees and desires, he touches and he dreams.

My flesh is sweet to him, and even in bed
My life exists for his life to be fed.

Zeno of Elea, in your cruelty,
With your winged arrow have you piercèd me?
It hums and flies, and yet it never moves:
The sound creates me, from the shaft I die.
Ah, sun . . . a tortoise-shadow for the soul,
Striding Achilles, motionless on high!

No, no, stand up! Into the coming age!
Awake, my body, break this cast of thought;
My breast, drink up the wind's returning power.
A sudden freshness, breathing from the sea
Restores my soul. . . . O saline potency!
Run to the waves and spring from them reborn!

Great sea tumultuous, your panther's skin
And flowing mantle woven through and through
With hundred-thousand facets of the sun;
Hydra in love with your own body's blue,
Biting your sparkling tail in clamour, yet
Your clamour and your silence are as one.

The wind is rising. . . . We must dare to live!
The vast air turns the pages of my book.
Against the rock the wave runs and is stripped,
Flung free in foam. Sun-blinded pages, scatter!
Break, waves, and with delighted water shatter
This quiet roof where once the dove-sails dipped.

Note. With regard to the sea as a 'roof', Valéry once remarked in a different context: "Most people see through their intellect far more often than
through their eyes. Instead of coloured spaces, they take note of concepts.
. . . Knowing the surface of still water to be horizontal, people fail to
realise that the sea is *upright* in the distance." *Les Divers Essais sur Léonard de
Vinci* (N.R.F., 1938), pp. 76–77

THE YOUNG FATE

A rendering of Valéry's *La Jeune Parque*

Who is it weeping, at this diamond hour,
Unless the wind? But who is it that keeps
So close to me, alone, and weeps?

Towards my brow the hand that dreaming strays,
Vaguely obedient to some profound end,
Looks to my weakness for a tear to start,
And to the slow parting of my ways
For purest light to pierce a ruined heart.
A shadow of reproach from where, below,
Murmurs the swell in rocky prison sunk;
Something complaining bitterly, as though
A draught of disillusion had been drunk.

Why do I tremble, icily distressed,
And why do shudders from a time forgotten
Run through the naked islands of my breast?
Craving disaster, dazzled, yet am I
Bound in my radiance to this unknown sky.

All-powerful strangers, stars immutable,
Deigning to lend to our mortality
I know not what supernal purity,
Into the heart you thrust, even to tears,

Your arms invincible, your sovereign spears,
The piercing raptures of eternity.
I am alone with you, at this vague time,
Trembling, aroused from rest, and marvelling:
What pain, I ask, has stirred my heart, what crime
By me committed or on me performed?
Or is it the evil of a dream rejected
When in the after-lamplight dusk I lay,
Buried my brow in folded arms and waited,
Searching my soul's dusk for break of day?
Yet am I mine, mistress of my own flesh,
A shiver tells me of its strange expanse;
Nursed in its blood, a willing prisoner, I
Have watched myself, with long exploring glance,
Illumine my deep forests. It is there
I followed the snake whose mark, whose bite, I bear.

Coils of desire . . . and O what disarray
Of cravings cheated, treasures wrenched away,
And yet an obscure thirst for clarity!

A trick! . . . In light of after-pain I saw
Myself exposed, not hurt so much as known . . .
One gleam of truth from my perfidious soul:
The poison of self-knowledge is my own.
It pricks with warmth a virgin's frigid cheek:
Jealous—of whom? And by whom threatened?
How to my one true self does silence speak?

Burns in my wound, O gods, a sister, she
Prefers her dark to bright, to light of me.

Away! I need no more your simple kind,
Dear Serpent . . . I grow dizzy in your coils!
Your sinuous proposals you may keep,
Your loyalty that claims to read my mind . . .
My soul can do without that ruinous light!
Casting its torments on my shadow-self, it knows
How well to nibble at my breasts by night
And suck the dreamy milk of paradise.
Your jewelled invitations, let them fall,
My spirit's destiny is not for love . . .
Your utmost action on me I would feel
Less cruel far, and less desirable . . .
So calm these waves, your backwash, and repeal
Your unclean promises, for now my eyes
Are open; I have finished with surprise.
From my rich solitude I looked for more
Than fever-fruit—but O its passionate depths
Glitter with dryness, however I explore
Its furthest range, and shame myself to find
The hopeless bounds of my sequestered mind.
I know . . . my lassitude can be a pose.
No spirit is so pure but catches fire
And with the flame of solitary desire
Burns through its dreary tomb. Who is content
To wait for endless nothing here below?
So then, with certain agony in store,

The craving soul opens the fiery door,
Admits the monstrous surge, the serpent-power . . .
And yet, however deft and swift you seem,
Capricious reptile, rippling with caresses,
Though patience falters and my burden presses,
What do you count in my eternal dream?
Careless you saw me, handsomely asleep,
But perils can be cheated where there's wit,
And craft, O Thyrsis, leaves the biter bit.
Back to the dark! Retrace your slimy tread!
Hatch out in other hearts their seeds of harm,
For slumberers keep your heavy dances and
Your shifting colours for some other bed,
And through the night let anxious innocence
Gasp in the coils of your concupiscence.
I—am awake. Pale and miraculous,
Humid with tears that I have never shed,
From mortal cradle, bathed in solitude,
Renouncing my serenity, I come,
And on one elbow poise my sovereign self.
All those my visions, through the night descried,
Shall yield their lightest impulse to my pride.

How could I bear to lose a sacred pain?
I kissed the small sharp tooth-marks on my hand,
Knew of my body lying there inert
Only as distant fire in a strange land.

Farewell, thou mortal sister, liar, ME. . . .

Harmonious ME, no image of a dream,
A woman firm and supple, whose pure acts
Follow her silences . . . Her limpid brow
And long light strands that wave and flow
And in the wind are wild. Come, say,
I was the compeer and the bride of day;
No other gave this loyalty of love
To the all-powerful radiance of the height. . . .

That brilliance on my lashes blind with light,
My eyelids treasure-laden, I would pray,
Sightless and groping in your golden night!
Swathed and pierced through by that eternal sky,
Offering my bloom to its devouring flame,
I had no impulse but a wish to die
In that bright softness for the sun to ripen:
It was before I tasted bitterness.
My naked shoulder only to the light
I sacrificed; and on that honeyed breast,
Whose tender birth the sky was nurturing,
The image of the world would sink to rest.
Then, a free captive in the god's bright power,
I trod the earth beneath his burning eye,
Weaving my shadow through the flax in flower.
A happy time! Responsive to my dress,
The stems I brushed would bow their fragile pride,
Their clustered heads. And when the less
Obedient briar laid sudden hold on me,

Tore at my dress and checked my liberty,
Then was my body's nakedness revealed,
Held taut against its summer drapery—
A flowery veil to match the flowering field!

This power, however vain, I half regret . . .
I was my own desire, obedient to
These satin limbs, whose swift responses met
My every wish—so instant-swift were they,
Almost ahead of thought they were away!
The radiance of my senses bathed my flesh
And in the ardent peace of my young dreams
With every step I touched eternity.
But at my feet, O Splendour, day by day,
The Enemy, my supple shadow, lay.
This withered image of the absent me
Across the earth without a trace would glide,
While from its light touch of death I fled.
Between the rose and me I saw it hide,
On dance of mortal dust it fell and passed,
Troubling no leaf, itself was scattered wide . . .
Glide on, funereal bark! . . .

                    . . . I am not dead,
But wide-awake, and hard, with secret strength
Drawn from my nothingness. But now, as though
One cheek alone by love were flushed with red,
One nostril only breathed the orange-flower,
I look on daylight with a stranger's glance . . .
How greatly could my curious night enhance
The hidden me, an alien to my heart,
And deepen through strange exercise my art! . . .

Far from the pure realms, a captive here,
Brought low by loss of that high-scented air,
I feel across my body shivers run,
A statue rippled over by the sun.
But well I know what once my dark eye saw:
Infernal regions lie beyond that door!
I think, while on the wind my hours
Are scattered, and that bitter scent of flowers;
Here on the golden border of the world
I think of her, the Pythoness, whose groan
Hopes for creation's ending, and her own.
My mysteries, my deities, return,
My footsteps hesitate, while to the skies
I speak, and while my waking dream
Mirrors the wing-beat of a bird that flies.
A hundred and a hundred times the sun
Plays with the abyss, and burns unspent,
His ardour on my yielding marble bent.

How perilous this focus of his gaze!

The spirit's eye has watched on silken shores
Brighten and turn to dusk so many days,
Their course and colour all too well foreknown;
This wearisome rehearsal of their ways
Gave me a deadly foretaste of my life:
With every dawn an enemy disclosed.
I was half dead, but with another half
Perhaps immortal, for my dream supposed
A future where my burning thoughts had come
Full circle, and in crystal cold were set,
Like diamond sadness round a coronet.

Will Time dare rescue from my various graves
A favourite evening and the sound of doves,
That evening which calls up a sudden flame,
Reflected from my docile childhood, and
Tempers in emerald dusk a rose of shame?

That memory is fire, whose golden breath
Brings crimson to the mask I will not wear,
Refusing to be other than I was . . .
Come, blood, and redden for me that pale year,
By distance azured, it was sanctified
And wore the halo of a time I loved!
Come and burn up in me this faded pride,
Come—let me recognise and hate to see
That moody child, that mute conspiracy,
That bathing with a shadow in the grove . . .
And from my frozen bosom hear again
The roughness of a voice oppressed by love . . .
The graceful throat of winged Diana dreaming.

Was I so close then to a heart so soon
To weaken, or were those long lashes mine
Which thought to snare me, careless of your threats,
In after-sweetness? On my cheek the vine
Spreading its tendrils, lingering in caress,
Or thou . . . of lashes and of willow woven,
The tender dusk with clinging arms confused.
"O let my eyes be open in the heights
To trace my temple, and on me alone

O may there rest its matchless altar-stone!"

So, marble-cold and pale, my body cried . . .
Nothing is left of earth but colours flowing
Up to the sheer white edge of vertigo . . .
I am the stem on which the universe
Trembles and sways: the crown of pensive thought
Eludes my spirit. Death desires to breathe
This rose without a price, whose sweetness tells
That soon it will be gathered into shade.

If I enthrall you with my scented air,
O hollow death, breathe in this royal slave:
Call me, release me . . . Bring me to despair,
So weary am I of my image self-condemned!
Listen . . . delay no more . . . the fresh new year
Speaks to my blood of secret changes near:
The frost lets fall its lingering diamonds . . .
Tomorrow, with a waft from friendly heaven,
Spring will unseal the fountains, break their bonds:
Astonishing spring, who comes to violate
With laughter—whence, who knows? But syllables
Ripple with voice so sweet and intimate,
Earth feels her entrails seized with tenderness . . .
The ripening trees swell out in summer dress,
Loaded with branches opening new horizons,
They move their thunderclouds against the sun,
Climb into pungent air with all their pinions,
Their million leaves in which they feel reborn.
Do you not hear these rustling aerial voices,
O deaf one! . . . While in branch-encumbered spaces
The living wood the lofty crest defies,

The tree entire pulled to and from the skies;
This floating forest through whose rugged members,
To where the splendid islands strain and sail—
Listen, O death—devotedly there passes
A tender stream, hidden below the grasses.
What mortal could resist this wave on wave?
A mortal, who?
             My knees, so pure am I
Tremble for fear of knees without defence . . .
The air undoes me. I am pierced by cry
Of birds like children, unimagined voice . . .
Heard in the shadow even where my heart
Is hidden, and my roses. You by sighs
Are stirred, my sighs: alas, the stronger part
Conquers the tender arms which shield the breast . . .
Oh, on my hair as soft as brush of bee,
Searching towards a kiss so heedless-sharp,
Delicious break of day, unsure for me . . .
The light! or death—whichever faster comes
May take me. But my heart, my heart is beating,
Fire in my bosom carries me away . . .
Grow large and hard, my breast, and tense—but say
That I am captive to that far blue height,
Yielding my hardness to its infinite.

Dear ghosts so nearly born, your thirst is mine,
Desires and shining faces! And then you,
Fair fruits of love, why did the gods imbue
My form with this maternal signature,
These curves and calices, when life will feed
On each delight in turn and force the soul,
A stranger to these endless coils of time,
To blend with flow of blood and milk and seed?
No—this is horror, loathsome harmony!

Each kiss presages a new agony . . .
Denied the pride of flesh I see them drift,
Millions of shades, bitter and impotent—
Whispers and glances, no, nor tenderness,
My guests impoverished, who entreat the gift
Of life from me—never from me! Away,
Spectres and sighs, breathed by the night in vain,
Go join the crowd of insubstantial dead!
No light to shadows will I grant. I stay
Far off from you, my spirit deadly clear,
Not from my lips the kindling flash . . . but then,
My heart witholds its thunderstroke—I must
Pity us all, frail eddies in the dust.

Great gods! In you I lose my troubled way!
Now for my only light, a little light,
I must entreat the tear that all but falls
To moist my cheek; no other answer comes.
This tear that veils before my trembling sight
The various ways to death, I speak to you.
From the soul's labyrinth, its heart of pride,
A drop of my dear essence come to hide
The sacrifice of shadows from my view—
Tender libation of my secret thought!
From hollow cave of fear far down in me
Mysterious salt exudes its speechless flow:
Where is your birthplace, tear, what travail sad
And always new compels you to this slow
Ascent from depth of bitter shade? Through me
As mortal and as mother, stage by stage,
You work your way and lacerate your road.
A lifelong time you linger, stubborn load,
And I am stifled. . . . But in silence I
Will drink your sure advance—Who calls you here?

Who bids you come to succour my young wound?

But wound and sobs and sad endeavours, why?
For whom, O cruel gems, do you invite
This frigid body, with blind fingers stretched
To fend off hope? Where heedless is it bound,
This ignorant body in the astonished night?
Uncertain earth . . . and seaweed, carry me,
Carry me gently . . . Limbs as weak as snow,
Will they walk on until the snare is found?
My drooping swan, where will it take its flight?

O precious firmness, signature of earth,
In you my steps had sacred confidence:
But when the living foot, feeling its way,
Touches with horror its own place of birth,
The firmness falters . . . And the path leads near
My dreaming precipice . . . The rocks are here,
Hard-natured, seaweed-wet, as lonely as
Oneself, and favourable to fall and flight . . .
And the wind weaves, as though across a shroud,
Confused sea-noises, waves in ruin loud,
And oars . . . So many hiccough sounds
And grating surges, shattered and renewed
From far at sea . . . The sparkling dice are tossed,
Scattered at random wildly, and are lost.

Who traces my bare feet, how long will he,
Alas, cease thinking of himself alone?
Uncertain earth, and seaweed, carry me!

Mysterious Me, so you are still alive!
Soon you will know yourself in morning light,
Sadly the same . . .
                         A mirror of the sea
Is rising . . . And its smile of yesterday,
By weary fading of the stars foretold,
Reflects pale lines of light across the cold
And stony east; gleams on the flooded prison
Where soon will float the circling far horizon . . .
See how in purity an arm shows bare.
Again, my arm, I see you . . . Dawn is here.

O rough awakening for a victim who
Is not a victim yet . . . This opening day,
So clear and sweet, and favoured by low tide
Fringing the level rocks; the swell has died.
My shadow leaves me, sacrifice intact,
Rosy with new desires, but bound upon
The fearful altar of my memories.
Out there, the foam is hardly to be traced,
And always there, with every turning wave,
A fisherman will balance in his boat.
So everything prepares its solemn act,
Always to rise again unique and chaste,
And to recover for the eager grave

A gracious air with laughter interlaced.

Divinities of rose and salt sea, hail!
Where the young light will first in glances fall . . .
You islands! Soon your reddening rocks the flame
Will touch with rumour of great paradise;
Above the fecund fire your peaks will rise—
O isles foreseen, your woods will thrive and sound
With beasts and thoughts and hymns of praise from men
On whom just heaven showers its gifts again.
You isles! Within the circuit of the seas,
Mothers, yet always virgin in my sight,
And Fates miraculous—down to the knees:
With flowers incomparable your air is sweet,
But in the depth how ocean-cold your feet!

Prepared behind the calmness of my brow,
My death, a secret child already late,
And you, those lofty scorns whereby I fled
So chastely from the lustre of my fate—
Was all this fervour more than transient?
None venturing nearer to the gods has dared
To bathe her forehead with their dazzling breath,
Seeking in shelter of the perfect dark
To invoke with whispered word the final height.

The brilliant pure prospect of death I bore
As once I had sustained the burning sun . . .
My desperate body offered its bare breast,
Wherein the soul, having drunk its fill of self,
Of silence and of glory and the rest,
Burdened to faintness by its memories,
Listens with hope to knocking on the wall—
This heart that strangely beats its life away,
At last enduring only by complaisance
A last leaf's quivering, my presence.

She cannot die who in her mirror wears
A pose of sadness, nourished by her tears.

O foolish one, I surely should have made
A marvellous end by choosing for my pain
To look on fickle chance with cool disdain!
A death more lucid will you ever find,
Or purer path whereon my sliding steps
Cling for the worse, than this long downward gaze
Of victim all exposed who pale, resigned,
Watches without regret her blood in flow,
No longer secret; little need she care.
In what blanched peace the purple leaves her now,
At the low tide of life and faintly fair!
Time's threatening wave she calms; no whiter could
The sovereign moment make her lily cheeks,

So close her flesh to sombre fountain bound! . . .
Always a further solitude she seeks . . .
And I—my heart was always nearer drawn
To such a fate; and dreamt of myself borne
In cypress shade towards a perfumed pyre,
Felt myself led and offered and consumed,
Promised entire to radiant clouds of joy!
Even I seemed to mingle with that tree
Whose majesty, dissolving far above,
To heaven's wide expanse is rapt in love.
Vastness receives me, and the incense fire
Breathes out in ever-reborn flame and flower
My heart's pure image . . . All the shining forms
Of human likeness in my essence tremble! . . .

No more! . . . Evoke no more that vanished hour!
Dark lily! Shadowy plaything of the skies,
Your virgin strength was not enough to break
A precious vessel . . . All those moments when
You touched the heights . . . But who could overpower
That power itself, impatient through your eyes
To contemplate the morning light which chose
To crown your forehead with its ardent rose?
Inquire and ask thyself by what blind course
The night has brought thee from among the dead
To light of day. Collect thyself and raise
Out of instinctive dark this thread
(Thy gleaming finger holds it from the sun).

This tenuous thread whose windings blindly followed
Have led thy life back to a morning shore . . .

Be subtle . . . cruel . . . yet more subtle! . . . Lie! . . .
But know! . . . And teach me by what magic lore
Thou cowardly one, who knew not how to fly
From thine own langorous breath, or from the spell
Of thine own bosom, with its scent of clay—
By what recoil, O reptile, hast thou found
To those sad-smelling caves thy backward way?

One night ago the deep and mistress flesh
Betrayed me . . . O, no dreams and no caress!
I was not tricked by demon or sweet air
With tempting fantasy of arms entranced
Round some strong neck, until they weakened there;
Nor was I brushed by feathers burning white:
The Swan-god was not near to me that night.

And yet he would have found a tender nest!
For in my virgin grace, with limbs close-pressed,
Shadowed I lay, a lovely offering . . .
But sleep and sweetness were too near embraced;
With hands in hollow of my hair enlaced,
To weakness I gave up my waking will.
Wrapped in my arms, another I became . . .
Who was it? Who took leave? Who passive lay?
Where did my melting heart forget its way?
What murmuring shell re-echoed my lost name?
How can I know the traitor tide whose ebb
Carried me from that pure extremity,
Too soon embraced, and gave me back a sigh?

Like bird with closing wings, I had to sleep.

It was the hour, perhaps, when in the mind
The seeress tires, becoming disinclined,
No longer what she was . . . A profound child
Vainly resists the unknown stages and
From far below for hands abandoned cries.
The supplications of the crownéd dead
One must obey, and learn to recognise
In passing breath a face . . .

                          Gently I come,
My brow at last in acquiescence bent;
My body I forgive, ashes I taste,
My happiness now only in descent:
Exposed to arms in pain, dark witnesses,
And stammered words, all round me, without end.
Sleep now, my wisdom. Make my absence thine;
Return alive to birth and innocence;
Accept the serpent-treasures of the deep.
Then sleep! Go down and sleep . . . and sleep.

*(A low and narrow way, gauze through a ring . . .
Laughter in death, those babbling voices, hark . . .
The bird drinks on thy lips and thou art blind . . .
Come down, speak low, the dark is not so dark . . .)*

          ★   ★   ★

Delicious shroudings, warm in disarray,
The bed where stretched and questioning I lay,
Where my heart's beating I resolved to still;
Almost a breathing tomb my dwelling was,
And over it the eternal listening will.
That place so full of me, imprinted there,
O hollow warmth and form of my own form,
With each return I knew you for my own:
And all that pride by your embrace brought down
To taste the degradation of a dream!
Marble between your folds, playing at death,
Reluctant idol now disposed for sleep,
A woman weary, ready yet to weep—
And then the enchanted caverns of her heart
And love that in her body lingered
Betrayed her yielding and her mortal part.
O archway secret, yet so near; that night
My raptures were to break thy isolation;
I did no more than nurse with sighs thy flanks
Where lay a morning promise of creation!
And now—with eyes by so much azure dazzled,
I watch unmoved the final fading star:
It seems those ancient torments were another's,
So perfectly the sun's young fire is burning
Regrets away, and with the dawn composes
The radiance of a body that was turning
Into the very substance of a tomb! . . .
Over the sea entire to where I stand
How lovely is the spreading of the sun!
I am still she who in thy breathing dwells,
My veil a shadow flying towards thy land. . . .

Were all my farewells, then, but dreams in vain,
Since I am living still? If now I come

Down to the shore, with garments rapt away,
To breathe without recoil the flying spray,
Drink with my eyes the smiling salt expanse,
Bracing myself against the wind's sharp play,
And on my face the summons of the sea:
If this great power drives on the furious surge,
Wave piled on wave, and thundering on the cape
The waters drown in white its monstrous shape
And vomit ocean deeps upon this rock,
From which the ice-drop dazzle leaps to bite
My tingling skin and touch my waking thoughts—
And then, and then, O sun, I must, in spite
Of all I was, adore the heart where thou
Hast come to know thyself, and I recover
The sheer delight of being born twice over.

Towards thy fire a virgin of the blood
Offers her gold-showered breast in gratitude!

APPENDIX

Paul Morphy has been regarded as possibly the most brilliantly gifted chess player of all time. This estimate may owe something to the brevity of his active career, and to the way in which his genius for the game stands out against the melancholy background of his life. We cannot tell whether he would have maintained his triumphant record over a long period, or how he would have fared against a modern master of close, positional play. But there is no doubt of the dazzling impression he made on his contemporaries.

He was born at New Orleans in 1837. At ten he learned the moves; at twelve he was a match for the best local players; a year later he more than held his own with visiting masters. In 1857, after qualifying as a lawyer, he won the first American chess congress in New York. Next year, aged twenty-one, he visited Europe. Having beaten all the best players he could find in London and Paris, he became virtual world champion by defeating the German champion, Adolf Anderssen, in a match of eleven games, winning seven, losing two and drawing two.

But in Europe he met with one serious disappointment which may have had a profound psychological effect on his later life. He had crossed the Atlantic in the hope of a match with the doyen of English players, Howard Staunton. On several occasions Staunton agreed to meet him, but in the end always made excuses; the match never came off.

On returning to New Orleans, Morphy issued a challenge, offering to give the odds of pawn and move to any player in the world. When this met with no response, he announced his retirement from public chess. He wished now to make a career as a lawyer, as his father had done, but he was hampered by his reputation as a chess prodigy, and by the Civil War. In later years he declined into a state of harmless paranoia accompanied by increasing aversion to chess; he died (apparently from a stroke) at the age of forty-four.

*   *   *

Of the various endeavours to interpret Morphy's early retirement and subsequent mental illness, the most searching is a paper by the late Ernest Jones, 'The Problem of Paul Morphy', read to the British Psycho-Analytical Society in 1930.[1] "It is plain," he remarks, "that the unconscious motive actuating the players is not the mere love of pugnacity characteristic of all competitive games, but the grimmer one of father-murder." (It seems that the old Persian *Shah-mat*—German *Schachmatt*, the equivalent of our check-mate—means literally 'the king is dead', or at least paralysed.) Now Morphy, Jones continues, could not have played chess with such supreme ease and confidence, or with such abnormal resistance to fatigue, unless in some way it provided "the best possible solution of any conflicts in the deepest trends of the personality. It follows that anything interfering with such an indispensable expression of the personality would be likely gravely to endanger its integrity, and so indeed events proved. Our knowledge of the unconscious motivation of chess-playing tells us that what it represented could only have been the wish to overcome the father in an acceptable way.[2] For Morphy, the conditions necessary for its acceptability were essentially three: that the act in question should be received in a friendly manner; that it should be ascribed to worthy motives; and that it should be regarded as a serious and grown-up activity. We shall see that each of these conditions was grossly violated on his fateful visit to Europe."

Dr. Jones quotes the opinion of Morphy's lifelong friend, Maurian, that Morphy "was never so passionately fond, so inordinately devoted to chess as is generally believed. . . . His only devotion to the game, if it may be so termed, lay in his ambition to meet and defeat the best players and great masters of this country and of Europe. He felt his enormous strength and never for a moment doubted the outcome."

[1] Published in Jones's *Essays in Applied Psycho-Analysis*, volume one (Hogarth Press, 1951). See also Philip W. Sergeant, *Morphy's Games of Chess* (New York, Dover Publications, Inc.; London, Constable; new edition, 1957)

[2] Morphy's father, with whom (as far as we know) he had always been on good terms, had died with unexpected suddenness in 1856; but his image, against which the son had to prove himself, would have remained fully alive and potent in Morphy's unconscious mind. "We may surmise," Dr. Jones says, "that his brilliant effort at sublimation was, like Shakespeare's *Hamlet* and Freud's *Traumdeutung*, a reaction to this critical event."

Among these European masters, Howard Staunton held, in Morphy's youthful eyes, a special place. He was in fact a father-figure, and by his repeated evasions of invitations to a match he frustrated Morphy's central purpose in visiting Europe. Morphy was disgusted also by the intrigues and jealousies he encountered in European chess circles, and mortified by implications that he was a professional chess player, concerned to make money out of the game—something he always refused to do. Finally, on his return home, he found that because of his chess triumphs, people refused to take him seriously as a lawyer. Through all these circumstances—and Staunton's refusals above all—a main outlet for the energies of his psyche was blocked. He turned away from chess and the seeds of his later paranoia were sown.

*　　*　　*

Dr. Jones makes out a good Freudian case for this interpretation of Morphy's personal tragedy; we are more immediately concerned here with some particular characteristics of his play.

In spite of his supreme confidence, his demeanour was always quiet and courteous. As a rule he played quickly, but never showed impatience if his opponent was slow. During a game he kept his eyes on the board; if he looked up at an opponent, it meant that the end was in sight. His physique was slight, but at chess he was tireless. He could play from early morning until midnight, day after day, with no sign of weariness or loss of form.

One remarkable episode is quoted by Dr. Jones from the testimony of F. M. Edge, who during part of Morphy's stay in Europe acted as his secretary and later published an account of it.[1] On this occasion, in Paris, Morphy played blindfold against eight strong opponents simultaneously. It took him ten hours to defeat them all and during the whole period he neither ate nor drank. At seven the next morning, after a good night's sleep, he called for Edge and dictated to him from memory the complete moves in all eight games, at the same time discussing all sorts of possible variations. "It will be agreed," Dr. Jones remarks, "that only a mind working with exceptional ease could have accomplished such an astounding feat."

[1] *The Exploits and Triumphs in Europe of Paul Morphy, the Chess Champion*, by Paul Morphy's late secretary (New York, 1859)

Morphy's favourite opening was the Evans Gambit, in which a pawn sacrifice is offered on the fourth move in order to give scope for rapid development. The prime importance of development— i.e. of obtaining early freedom of action for the major pieces—was the great lesson taught by Morphy to many of his victims. Whenever he could, he played for attack, often clearing the way for it with a sacrifice. The most famous of these sacrificial combinations (though the game was not one of Morphy's best) occurred during his match with Paulsen in New York in 1857, shortly before his visit to Europe. Paulsen (White) played the Four Knights opening, and after Paulsens's 17th move the following position was reached:

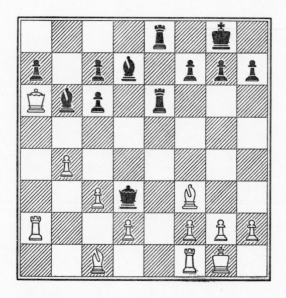

Morphy then played 17 . . . Q × B, offering to sacrifice his Queen for the Bishop. "Paulsen", Dr. Jones writes, "was naturally suspicious of a trap and carefully investigated the possibilities. After pondering on the situation for more than an hour, and detecting no trap, he accepted the offer, and after eleven more moves had to resign." The game went:

Paulsen	Morphy
18 P × Q	R — Kt3 *ch.*
19 K — R1	B — R6
20 R — Q1	B — Kt7 *ch.*
21 K — Kt1	B × P *dis. ch.*
22 K — B1	B — Kt7 *ch.*
23 K — Kt1	B — R6 *dis. ch.*
24 K — R1	B × P
25 Q — B1	B × Q
26 R × B	R — K7
27 R — R1	R — R3
28 P — Q4	B — K6

White resigns.

"Years afterwards," Dr. Jones continues, "Steinitz carried out a full analysis of the situation and maintained as a result of it that the future possibilities of the game were far too numerous and complicated for it to be conceivable that any human brain could calculate and predict them. It so happened that an onlooker had asked Morphy after the game was over whether he had been able to foresee the end of it from the famous move; to the question he returned the enigmatic answer: 'I knew it would give Paulsen a deal of trouble'."

★   ★   ★

Morphy was by no means infallible, of course; his games have been exhaustively studied and errors found even in some of those he won. Other great chess players have been equally precocious, have brought off equally brilliant sacrificial combinations, have surpassed his feats of blindfold play. No one else has risen to the front rank so quickly or with so little experience behind him, but the competition in those days was hardly comparable with what it later became. Morphy's truly unique characteristic, perhaps, was his quiet but boundless confidence. The Revd. G. A. MacDonnell, who watched him play in London, wrote: "I fancy he always discerned the right move at a glance, and only paused before making it, partly out of respect for his antagonist and partly to certify himself of its correctness, to make assurance doubly sure, and to accustom himself to sobriety of demeanour in all circumstances."[1]

[1] *Chess Life-Pictures* (London, 1883)

Well, this cannot be literally true, or Morphy would never have lost a game. But to observers it did seem that he must have a special gift for seizing the essentials of a position with very little expenditure of time or trouble. It could be that he was fairly often prompted by intuitions derived from his having exceptional—but almost certainly unconscious—access to the relations-pattern which the sight of a position had set up somewhere in his mind.[1]

[1] Since writing this Appendix I have read Vladimir Nabokov's novel, *The Defence* (Weidenfeld and Nicolson, 1964) about a chess grandmaster, Luzhin. The following passage seems relevant to some of J's experiences, described in my Chapter X:

"Luzhin was indeed tired. Lately he had been playing too frequently and too unsystematically; he was particularly fatigued by playing blind, a rather well-paid performance that he willingly gave. He found therein deep enjoyment: one did not have to deal with visible, audible, palpable pieces whose quaint shape and wooden materiality always disturbed him and always seemed to him but the crude, mortal shell of exquisite, invisible chess forces. When playing blind he was able to sense these diverse forces in their original purity. He saw then neither the Knight's carved mane nor the glossy heads of the Pawns—but he felt quite clearly that this or that imaginary square was occupied by a definite, concentrated force, so that he envisioned the movement of a piece as a discharge, a shock, a stroke of lightning—and the whole chess field quivered with tension, and over this tension he was sovereign, here gathering in and there releasing electric power."

INDEX

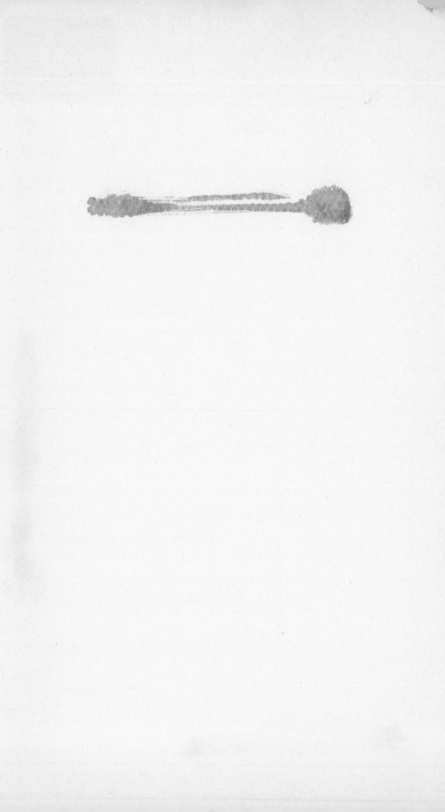